For little Aashi

whose *bhalonam* is Arushi

JHUMPA LAHIRI'S

The Namesake

A Critical Study

JHUMPA LAHIRI'S

The Namesake

A Critical Study

Jagdish Batra

Prestige

an international publishing house

Published by

Prestige Books International

New Delhi 110060

email: prestigebooks@gmail.com

Printed in India

Contents

Additional Perspectives

Preface

The phenomenal growth taking place presently in the field of Indian Writing in English, particularly in the genre of novel, is attributable mainly to the initiative taken by our diasporic writers. Salman Rushdie is generally credited with having blazed the trail with his *Midnight's Children* in 1981. Since then there have been many, at home and abroad, who have shown the might of their pen and won laurels. They include leading lights like Amitav Ghosh, Rohinton Mistry, Vikram Seth, Kiran Desai et al as also the not-so-prominent ones like Indra Sinha, Ruchir Joshi, Manil Suri and others. The last decade of the twontieth century is replete with many success stories. My estimate is that even after the turn of the century, more than a hundred novels of good calibre have been published. This has, quite naturally, enriched the genre of Indian English novel.

Jhumpa Lahiri, who won the Pulitzer Prize in the year 2000 for her *Interpreter of Maladies,* is a brilliant novelist. Along with Salman Rushdie and Arundhati Roy, she is looked upon as the harbinger of the new wave in Indian fiction. Her first novel *The Namesake* forms the basis of the present study. Lahiri has the first-hand experience to authentically portray the diasporic experience of the second generation of immigrants in America. At the same time, she has taken pains to imagine the experience of loss and nostalgia of the first generation immigrants also.

This book has been prepared to help the postgraduate and research students of Indian universities. Different dimensions of the novel including various themes, characterization, stylistic aspects etc. have been dealt with in detail. Apart from a critical summary, some research papers on *The Namesake* have also been included in this book, which should be of special interest to researchers. I am thankful to Prof. R.K. Dhawan who provided me the initial impetus to undertake this venture. Also I stand obliged to the contributors—Prof. S.L. Paul, a great scholar and philosopher, Dr. Santwana Haldar, well-known critic and writer, Sagar Pandya, an experienced academic as also Dr. Tanushree Singh, whose doctoral research centres on Jhumpa Lahiri.

JAGDISH BATRA
jagdishbatra@rediffmail.com

Chapter 1

Jhumpa Lahiri and Her Works

Jhumpa Lahiri has carved out a niche for herself among the contemporary popular novelists. She belongs to the second generation of immigrants to America and therefore, she can very well comprehend the plight of young generation that feels sandwiched between the aspirations of parents cast in the traditional Indian mould and the influence of the western peer groups as also of the wider American milieu. In an interview given to Rachel Hore, Jhumpa Lahiri admits, "I write about people whose very existence has been shaped by unsettlement."

Jhumpa was born Nilanjana Svadeshna on July 11, 1967 in London. Her parents are of Indian origin. Later in 1969, the family, moved to America where her father took up a job as a librarian in a university in the Rhode Island. It was here that she grew into a young woman. She travelled several times to India because of the family links. A number of stories in *Interpreter of Maladies* are set in Calcutta. She did her graduation in English literature from Barnard College. Later, she studied at Boston University and got several degrees—M.A. in English, M.A. in Creative Writing, M.A. in Comparative Studies in Literature and the Arts, and a Ph.D. in Renaissance Studies. In this way, she proved her credentials as an accomplished intellectual. She took up teaching as a career thereafter. She has taught creative writing at Boston University and at the Rhode Island School of Design.

She shot to fame with her first collection of short stories titled *Interpreter of Maladies* which won her the Pulitzer Prize 2000 for Fiction. She also bagged the *New Yorker* Prize for the Best First Book in addition to the PEN/Hemingway Award. A winner of the Henfield Prize from the Transatlantic Review, she has published stories in *The New Yorker, Agni, Story Quarterly* etc. *The Namesake* is her first novel and has been followed by *Unaccustomed Earth*, another collection of short stories. *The Namesake* is one of the national bestsellers and has been named as the 'Best Book of the Year' (2003) by the *USA Today*. Based on this novel, the film of the same name directed by Mira Nair was released internationally in February, 2007.

Talking about her early life, Lahiri feels that her childhood was not happy. Her experience differed from her parents because they belonged to India. Their experience as immigrants in other countries was not a happy one but then they could think of their home and find support in those musings. On the other hand, she comments, "My and my sister's upbringing was almost hydroponic because our roots had nowhere to cling. . . . When I go back to New England now, I do feel a sense of return. It was where I was raised" (Hora). Presently, she lives in Brooklyn with Alberto Vourvoulias Bush, her Guatamlian-American husband, who is a senior editor of a leading Spanish daily. She has two small children.

The collection of short stories *Interpreter of Maladies* (1999) has the further explanatory sub-title: 'Stories of Bengal, Boston and Beyond.' The popularity of this book can be gauged from the fact that it has been translated into no fewer than 29 languages of the world. (Sherif) These are simple and touching stories beautifully crafted around common themes. The condition of the diasporic is the constant concern of Jhumpa Lahiri. India is a strong presence in the nine stories contained in this collection. Most of these stories appeared earlier in *The New Yorker* and other publications. She can be easily compared to Anita Desai in her comprehension of the cultural chasm dividing the two communities, even though she is not gifted with the smooth, poetic prose of Desai. Her characters are the children of postmodern times, so they do not recognize boundaries of any type—political, social or cultural. When it comes to the pursuit of love, even the generational difference is sought to be glossed over.

The lead story 'Interpreter of Maladies' is a long story covering twenty-seven pages. An interpreter guides an American family through India, which is the land of their forefathers. The Das couple is a specimen of marital discord. Mrs. Das is bored of her life in New York because she has not much to do when her husband is gone to work. Mr. Das does not have time to share with his wife and understand her sentiments. What follows is Mrs. Das's infatuation for her driver Mr. Kapasi. As they travel by car to the Sun Temple in Orissa, they come so close to each other that Mrs. Das tells the driver that Bobby, her son, is actually born of her union with a Punjabi friend of her husband who had stayed with them for a week. The driver is not able to understand as to why she has confided in him so easily and he does not take interest in her story. Mrs. Das is peeved at this reaction and shouts at him to understand her situation. She lays bare her state of mind which shows she is suffering from the malady of being unwanted, uncared in an alien country. Thus, he is expected to be the interpreter of maladies. The novel relies heavily on details of situations and places in order to delineate characters.

Lahiri's first novel *The Namesake* was published in 2003. It deals with the life of an Indian immigrant family over the period 1968 to 2000 A.D. It begins with the traditional scene in Indian families where the family of the prospective groom is invited to the girl's home to negotiate the matrimonial alliance. The ritual bears fruit and Ashoke and Ashima are tied in wedlock. For the young couple, life starts in Cambridge, U.S.A. where Ashoke is doing research at the MIT. Soon the couple is blessed with their first baby—a boy named Gogol. Years ago in India, Ashoke's life was saved following a nasty train accident simply because the rescue party noticed him through the movement of a few pages of the book—a collection of stories by the famous Russian writer Nikolai Gogol—held in the hands of a semi-conscious Ashoke. So, the writer Gogol's name got etched on Ashoke's mind as his saviour. Even so, he would not have named his child Gogol had the letter sent by his grandmother suggesting a name for the newborn—she had always given names to her progeny—had arrived in time. In fact, the letter got lost in transit between India and the U.S.A. and in order to meet the requirement of the hospital where the child was born, the child had to be named then and there and the name 'Gogol' came in handy.

However, as the child grew, he was made to see the absurdity of the name by his American friends and class-mates and he started hating it. Finally, when he turned eighteen, Gogol officially changed his name to Nikhil. However, this change too, did not prove to be a smooth affair and it entailed identity problem for him. Somehow, the name Gogol continued to stick to him and this neither-American-nor-Indian appendage became a symbol of his struggle with identity, culture and everything en route.

His father Ashoke took up the job of a professor outside Boston. But for Gogol and others of his generation, mixing up with Americans of their age did not pose any problem. He had a series of affairs, starting with his first girl-friend Ruth. After a minor quarrel, Gogol shifted to New York where he worked as an architect. It is here at a party that he met Maxine with whom he had a serious affair. She had had a break-up already and her parents were quite liberal. However, Gogol's father died unexpectedly. Gogol was so much affected by it, or rather by the guilt complex over his disinterestedness in his own family till then that he refused to leave his home and settle down with Maxine. The result was a break-up again.

Thereafter, Ashima got in touch with the Mazoomdars, her family friends who had a daughter of marriageable age and arranged a meeting between Gogol and Moushumi. She was an ultra-modern girl who, like Gogol, also hated Bengali culture. This initiative of the parents bore fruit and both got married in the traditional Bengali style. But Moushumi's interests were different. She was a free bird who hated restrictions of any type. In the past also, she had been ready to sleep with any guy at the drop of a hat. Her unfaithfulness led to the undoing of her marriage. In the end, Ashima is seen to follow in the footsteps of her late husband who had been inspired by the life history of his favourite writer Nikolai Gogol as also by a fellow-traveller in the train to pack up his bag and set out to see the world. Ashima decides to spend six months in India practising singing, something that had always attracted her and the remaining six months in America with her children. At a point of time, her resolve seems to shake but then Gogol bucks her up.

Lahiri is a painstaking writer which is reflected in her laboured prose that tries to create a balance between the internal and the external details, between the landscape and the mindscape. She has been taken note of in the literary world and estimates of her as a writer range from comparison with the likes of Virginia Woolf and Jane Austen to the creator of a "buttoned-down world in which much is documented but little revealed" (Kirkus). This novel has also been filmed by the celebrated film-director Mira Nair, although some changes have been made in this adaptation.

In 2008 appeared *Unaccustomed Earth,* a collection of eight stories. The locale covers a wide area from Cambridge and Seattle to India and Thailand. Through these stories, the secrets at the heart of family life are sought to be explored through a mélange of relationships—brothers and sisters, fathers and mothers, daughters and sons, friends and lovers. They grow up in America, marry non-Indians but cannot escape the burden of family traditions. Siddharth Dhanvant Shanghvi calls it a "scandalously brilliant collection."

The lead story 'Unaccustomed Earth' revolves around a woman who is worried that after the death of her mother, she would have to take care of her father and ask him to stay with her family at Seattle. She is possessed by such thoughts when her father comes to stay with her for a couple of days. However, there is no hint from her father that he needs to be taken care of. Instead, he gets busy with setting up her garden and it is only in the end that she realizes he has plans of his own and never intended to stay with her forever.

The story 'Nobody's Business' details a failed affair in which the protagonist Sang Biswas is betrayed by her lover. She fails to come up to the expectations of her parents who wanted her to do Ph.D. at Harvard. In another story, 'Only Goodness,' an alcoholic wrecks his sister's trust by putting in danger her son's life. Another story titled 'Hell-Heaven,' which is the shortest and perhaps the most touching one in the collection, we find a young Bengali mother, Aparna, who welcomes a young and hungry Bengali bachelor student into her kitchen. She gets attached to him at first and then resents the young man's new girlfriend. The depth of her despair becomes clear years later only when she has already overcome it.

The last three stories forming the second part turn the book into a kind of continued novella about the lives of the two main characters—a girl named Hema and a slightly older boy called Kaushik, both of whom have been raised in America to their respective Bengali parents. They are members of a jazz troupe. As children, they meet through their families who know each other. Kaushik and his family are hosted temporarily by Hema's family while they look for a new house in the neighborhood. Kaushik, much against his family's injunction, confides in Hema a secret. In the second story, Kaushik's father remarries a younger woman after his wife's death which comes as a blow to Kaushik who loved his mother much. In the third story, they meet again in Italy. Thus, taken together, the three stories trace the characters' lives through his mother's early death to cancer, his father's remarriage, and the careers of both—Hema and Kaushik.

Praising Lahiri's art of characterization, Siddhartha Shanghvi feels that these are not lightly drawn as in the *Interpreter of Maladies*. He talks about ancient seekers, who lived in sight of both worlds, but looked towards the unknown. "The characters in Lahiri's work are exactly that, border-dwelling ballet dancers, elegantly tiptoeing around beautiful broken glass of life," he comments.

Chapter 2

The Namesake: A Brief Summary

The story begins in 1968, when Ashoke Ganguli and his wife, Ashima, newly married according to the Indian arranged marriage system, arrive at Cambridge, U.S.A., where Ashoke was a doctoral candidate in electrical engineering at the MIT. Whereas Ashoke looked forward to fulfilling his ambition in the land of promise, Ashima found it a kind of exile, away from her kith and kin. Passing time on the alien soil was a big problem but somehow she got used to it. Soon, she conceived and gave birth to a baby boy.

As the baby grew into a school-going child, there emerged a problem. The name 'Gogol' was given to the child haphazardly. The hospital needed a name for the birth certificate before Ashima could be discharged and Ashoke could think only of his favourite Russian writer Nikolai Gogol at that crucial moment. He thought he was giving his child a temporary name—a *daknam* to be used at home only as is the practice in Bengal and that when the child goes to school, he will be given the proper name—a *bhalonam* at that time.

Actually, Ashima's old grandmother was to select the proper name for the child. She did send a letter suggesting the name but the letter got lost en route and in the meantime, the grandma went off her mind due to an accident. Nobody had been taken into confidence by her so that the grandma's choice was never known.

In a flashback, it is revealed that there is more to this name because it is connected to a near-fatal train accident in which Ashoke was involved before he got married. Actually, on his way to visit his grandfather in Jamshedpur, Ashoke was reading his favourite story, Nikolai Gogol's 'Overcoat,' contained in the collection *The Short Stories of Nikolai Gogol*, when his train got derailed. Lying amid the wreckage and clutching some pages of his book, Ashoke was almost taken for dead, but he managed to wave the torn page of the book meekly. This movement was noticed and he was rescued. It was like a second span of life for him, for which he felt obliged to Nikolai Gogol! Thereafter, he got married to Ashima and moved to America.

As the Gangulis prospered and moved to the suburbs, Gogol grew up absorbing the American culture and values like other children of his age in the school. By the time Gogol reached the age of five, he also had a sister who was named Sonia. The important issue for any Indian immigrant parents is the acculturation of their children. Both Gogol and Sonia were occasionally taken to attend classes in Hindu culture as also to celebrations of Hindu festivals. There were get-togethers of Bengali friends of the Gangulis at their house. But they also celebrated Christmas and Thanksgiving. Thus, the children were sought to be introduced to Indian culture without their feeling alienated from American friends.

Gogol's parents regularly visited Calcutta to keep in touch with their relatives there. Once they spent eight months in India. The children, brought up in America at that impressionable age, had a hard time getting adjusted to the Indian milieu. On his fourteenth birthday, Gogol was presented Nikolai Gogol's *The Short Stories of Nikolai Gogol* by his father but he did not read it and dumped the book in a corner.

Meanwhile, Gogol faced problems because of his odd name which was neither American nor Bengali, but Russian, and a last name at that. His class-mates teased him about it. And so, entering Yale after completing his school education, he changed his name to Nikhil. He also took to youthful habits like smoking pot sometimes and flirting with girls. Meanwhile, his father Ashoke had done well and was appointed professor of electrical engineering at the university.

As Nikhil, he studied architecture and began his career in New York. He had several relationships with girls. Ruth was his first regular girl-friend though when she moved to England to study, the connection got severed. His second girlfriend was Maxine. Her parents—Gerald Ratliff and Lydia Ratliff—lived life that was poles apart from that of the Gangulis. Nikhil (Gogol) marked this contrast on many an occasion. He had the opportunity to vacation in their company at their house by the lake, away from the city. The house provided for bare necessities only but there was plenty of land to grow vegetables. The Ratliffs passed time idly and cosied up even in the presence of Gogol. They did not mind Gogol's staying with their daughter in the same room. This relationship lasted for a long time but came to an end some months after Gogol's father died of heart attack. Maxine tried to extract Gogol out of grief but he was so overwhelmed by it that he wanted to devote himself only to look after his mother.

Gogol's mother was now concerned about finding a bride for her son. She got him to meet Moushumi, whose parents were the family friends of the Gangulis. Both of them liked each other and got married later in a typical Bengali manner. They had many memories of their teenage years to share. They had met earlier on the get-togethers organized at Gogol's home. She was doing Ph.D. in French at the university. Later, she also visited Paris on account of a seminar. Gogol also went with her even though he had no business of his own there and had to pass time somehow. At a party at a friend's house, she unwittingly blurted out the secret that Gogol (now known as Nikhil) had actually changed his name. Gogol did not like it. By and by, differences started cropping up between Gogol and Moushumi.

Moushumi's first wedding anniversary was memorable because she had cleared her ABD, which meant she had now only to submit her dissertation for the Ph.D. in French. Moreover, she got a teaching assignment for one year in France. There, the streak of independence in her character asserted itself and she indulged in some harmless activities to assure herself that she was master of her own self.

After completing her work in France, she joined New York University as a teacher. One day, she happened to lay her hands on a letter addressed to another professor from an old acquaintance of hers—Dimitri. She had had a fling on him during her school days. So, sheer curiosity forced her to trace the writer of the letter which led to sexual relationship with Dimitri. As had been her wont, she overdid it. In a week, she would go to his apartment three times. One day, while discussing the place where they would be celebrating Christmas, an unguarded comment by Moushumi blew the lid off the affair and that was the end of their married life.

In the end, we find Gogol alone, planning to set up his own firm in New York. His sister is to get married to Ben, a Frenchman. Their mother Ashima decides to take up a roving life—spending six months in India and the remaining six in America. In this way, she would be fulfilling the condition of permanent displacement, the hallmark of a diasporic. At a party thrown by Ashima prior to her leaving for India, Gogol discovers the book *The Short Stories of Nikolai Gogol* that had been lying unnoticed in his room. He started reading it now with a renewed understanding and interest. Through all his efforts to find an identity as Nikhil, the protagonist remains Gogol at home. He knows now that his father's attachment to the name ran deeper than mere literary affection.

Chapter 3

The Namesake: A Detailed Critical Summary

It is the story of a Bengali couple and their children living in the U.S.A. Ashoke Ganguli is studying for his Ph.D. in electrical engineering at the MIT (Massachusetts Institute of Technology) situated in the city of Cambridge (not to be confused with Cambridge in England) in the Massachusetts state of America. As the novel begins, we find that his wife Ashima is expecting her first child. Therefore, she is admitted to Mount Auburn Hospital.

Once at the hospital, Ashima feels lonely even though there are three other pregnant women—all Americans—in the same room, separated by curtains. She is aware of the concern for privacy in Americans. She has, therefore, no option but to reflect on her own life. She arrived in America eighteen months ago. She has been concerned about delivering her child on foreign soil "unmonitored, unobserved by those she loved" (6). Her flawed English is noticed by the nurse Patty when she says 'finger and toe' for 'fingers and toes' because in Bengali language, the plural form is not different from the singular.

Match-Making Recalled

Ashima's thoughts go back to her past life in Calcutta. She remembers, in particular, the day when Ashoke had visited her house as a prospective groom. The camera of Ashima's consciousness now zooms in on Ashoke's brown leather shoes with black heels and off-white laces which he had taken off to enter Ashima's home as is the custom in India. A childish impulse overtook her as she tried fitting her foot into these strange shoes. Lying in the hospital bed, the entire scene of the first introduction to her would-be husband comes to her mind. The parents generally try to extol the virtues of their marriageable children. How her mother had falsely bragged about her domestic skills to impress Ashoke brings a smile to her face. "She [Ashima] is fond of cooking, and she can knit extremely well. Within a week she finished this cardigan I am wearing," her mother had said. (7)

Ashima was asked routine questions like whether she was willing to live in a city that had severe winters and which reeled under snow to which she responded with the innocent question while pointing to Ashoke, "Won't he be there?" (9). As is common in such cases, the marriage ceremony did not take long to be solemnized and when she left in the company of her husband for America, there were as many as twenty six relatives on the Dumdum airport to see her off. She had reached eight thousand miles away from her home to Cambridge, where she settled down to a routine in which her role was traditional—to wait for her husband to return from the university and to cook food for him.

The Train Accident

As Ashima was taken into the operation theatre for delivery, Ashoke paced the hospital floor reading the *Globe*. We are told that he had been an avid reader as a bachelor. His grandfather, a former professor of European literature at the Calcutta University, used to read to him the English translations of his favourite Russian writers Dostoyevsky and Tolstoy. We also come to know of a near fatal accident that occurred in Ashoke's life. He was a student at B.E. College and was travelling by the 83 Up Howrah-Ranchi Express train from Calcutta to Jamshedpur to be with his grandfather. His grandfather had retired and had also lost vision to a great extent. He wanted Ashoke's company. In the train compartment, Ashoke had the company of a Bihari couple and a middle-aged Bengali businessman Mr. Ghosh, who tried to impress upon Ashoke the need to see the outside world: "Do yourself a favour, pack a pillow and a blanket and see as much of the world as you can. You will not regret it. One day it will be too late," he said (16). He also gave him his address in case Ashoke went abroad and needed contacts. Ashoke, thereafter, buried himself in the study of a volume of short stories by the Russian writer Nikolai Gogol. His favourite story was 'The Overcoat.'

The train was at a distance of 209 kilometers from Calcutta, when suddenly, there was a huge sound as if of a bomb blast, following which the train was derailed. It was said that some fishplates had been removed but it was never confirmed. Some coaches capsized while others telescoped into each other, killing many passengers in their sleep. Ashoke himself was trapped in the mangled coach. There were bodies of dead and injured people around him. Blood and dust was all about him. At early dawn, help arrived and he was able to catch the attention of a rescuer not by shouting, as he was too weak, but by waving a page of the book he had been reading. Thus, Gogol's collection of short stories proved to be his saviour.

He was taken to the hospital where it was found that he had broken his pelvis, his right femur and three of his ribs. For the next year, he lay flat on his back—first three months in different hospitals and then at home. The next year, he returned to his college and graduated. He then applied for engineering studies abroad without taking anybody in the family in confidence. Despite protests from his parents and siblings, he reached U.S.A., all of which marks him as a person of strong will. This happened seven years ago and the terrible thoughts of the accident still overpower him at times.

2. Gogol's Birth

This chapter introduces the protagonist of the novel, viz., Gogol, the son of Ashoke and Ashima. He is the namesake of the famous Russian writer Nikolai Gogol. Ashima is in the hospital. Her labour pains got prolonged and it was only the next morning that the child—a baby boy—was born. The chapter describes in detail the feelings of Ashoke and Ashima who have become parents for the first time. Patty, the nurse, is of great help to them as they start learning the art of parenting. Maya and Dilip Nandi visit them in the hospital. They are a young married couple who were befriended by the Gangulis a few months ago. Similarly, Dr. Gupta, a bachelor in his fifties, who also works at the MIT, also visits them. Ashoke and Ashima miss their family on this happy occasion and feel America is "only half true" for them (25).

Ashoke telegraphically informs his as well as Ashima's families in India about the birth of the child. They now wait for the christening of the baby because the name has to be suggested by Ashima's grandmother. It is their way of according honour to the old matriarch. But the wait remains endless, for the letter written by the grandmother fails to reach them and in the meantime, the old lady goes off her mind due to an accident. She never told anyone about her choice of name for the newborn. Since it is compulsory to give the baby a name before leaving the hospital, Ashoke comes up with 'Gogol,' the name of his favourite author. So, the baby is registered as Gogol Ganguli after which they leave the hospital.

The Gangulis live now in a three-room apartment. The top two floors are occupied by the landlord Prof. Montgomery who lives with his wife Judy and two daughters Amber and Clover, aged seven and nine respectively. The professor is least bothered about his dress and his house is always in a mess. In comparison, the Gangulis are methodical in keeping their place clean but during Ashima's stay at the hospital, Ashoke has also not been able to keep the flat tidy. Now that Ashima has returned from the hospital, the landlord's family arrives and they celebrate their homecoming with the uncorking of a bottle of champagne.

Ashima would like her husband to finish his studies at the earliest so that they can go back to India. There are many passages in the novel that are devoted to the description of Ashima crying often as she feels lonely and without support in looking after the child. Their circle of acquaintance grows. The Nandis, the Mitras and the Banerjees are introduced. Their gatherings on holidays are roaring affairs. One such get-together is devoted to Gogol's *annaprasan* ceremony. Life goes on as the bachelor Bengalis in their circle of acquaintance visit India to get married.

American Honesty

Once Ashima goes shopping and while travelling by train on her way back, forgets her shopping bags in the train. She is very upset but Ashoke comforts her. He contacts the MBTA Lost and Found department on phone. The bags are retrieved and delivered to them intact; there is not a single item missing. This aspect of American life impresses Ashima very much and she talks about it on many occasions in the days that follow. The chapter concludes with the news of the death of Ashima's father reaching them. They leave for India six days later.

3. Gogol's Schooling Begins

The Gangulis shift to a university town outside Boston, for Ashoke is an Assistant Professor of Electrical Engineering at the University now, something to which he had aspired all his life. Starting with his nursery school, Gogol's growth is described in detail. The chapter also contains descriptions of 'yard sales' in America, where goods are sold cheap and the immigrant community makes full use of the opportunity. As Gogol turns five, Ashima delivers a baby girl who is christened Sonia. More births and deaths among relatives in India are reported. Gogol is sent to a Bengali class also so that he learns about his parents' native culture.

Gogol is admitted to a kindergarten school. His name causes problem at school because his parents want his name changed to Nikhil. This would be his good name, they explain to the Principal but she is not able to understand the difference between a name meant to be used at home and another to be used in school records because such a double-name scheme is not practised in America. When the Principal addresses the child as 'Nikhil,' he is unable to respond. Therefore, after the parents are gone, she enters the pupil's name as Gogol in the registration form.

A field trip for the school children to a graveyard causes consternation to Ashima, who is not able to appreciate the logic of the trip. In India, such a visit would not be considered proper, more so for the children of Gogol's age-group. However, Gogol was curious to find familiar names on the tombstones. When he did not find any, he grew sad. He did copy the epitaphs by rubbing crayons on the sheet put on the gravestone as the other children did and brought his work home. Gogol insisted that his mother put up the rubbings alongside his sketches in the kitchen, but his mother would have none of it. Finally, he took them upstairs to his room and put them in his room.

4. Teenager Gogol

Gogol is now fourteen-year old boy. At the birthday party Gogol is unable to find friends of his age except one—Moushumi. His father presents him *The Short Stories of Nikolai Gogol*. He would have preferred some other book. It is also discovered that by now, "he's come to hate questions pertaining to his name, hates having constantly to explain. He hates having to tell people that it doesn't mean anything 'in Indian'" (76). He even hates to wear the nametag on his sweater at school function because to him, it is absurd and obscure and has nothing to do with anything Indian or American. He is particularly peeved that his parents chose, even among the Russians, "the weirdest namesake" (76). There were other Russian names like Leo, Anton or Alexander, which he would have rather preferred. He has often told his father that Gogol was not his favourite author. He rues his first day at the kindergarten when he could have been Gogol "only fifty percent of the time. Like his parents, when they went to Calcutta, he could have had an alternative identity, a B-side to the self" (76).

He is almost six feet tall now. His voice has begun to deepen and his Adam's apple is prominent. He casually goes through the book presented to him by his father and notes that the writer's first name was Nikolai. Ashoke tells him about the importance of the novelist, saying that he spent most of his adult life outside his homeland like him but when he is about to refer to the train accident, he stops because, "his son's birthday, is a day to honour life, not brushes with death" (78). After Ashoke has gone, Gogol has a different perception of his name. Now, he thinks that not only does he have a "pet name turned good name, but a last name [of the author Nikolai Gogol] turned first name" (78). And so it occurs to him that no one in the world shares his name which is Gogol Ganguli. This should bring some kind of self-confidence to him.

Visiting India

The family goes to India for eight months, far too long for the children. In India they enjoy the hospitality of their numerous relatives. This gives Jhumpa Lahiri the opportunity to describe the Bengali lifestyle. The problems like lawlessness in trains are also pictured. The writer describes their departure thus: "At the airport the row of people who had greeted them, have hosted and fed and fawned over them for all these months, those with whom he shares a name if not his life, assemble once more on the balcony, to wave good-bye" (86).

Back in America, they feel disconnected. Meanwhile, Gogol is growing like any other American teenager, for the impact of environment proves to be greater than that of inheritance. Howsoever hard the parents might believe him to be shy and innocent, the fact is that he has started experimenting secretly with what are considered taboos among Indians. He has smoked pot, freaked out with companions to dance parties and would soon experience what is called loss of virginity.

5. Gogol becomes Nikhil

Gogol is serious about changing his name to Nikhil and for that purpose he initiates legal proceedings. After all, tens of thousands of Americans changed their names every year. The change of name is granted and Gogol becomes Nikhil. He lets his friends and acquaintances know the new name. His parents also try steadily to change their way of addressing their son as Nikhil, which, of course, gives birth to strange feelings in him. "But now that he's Nikhil it's easier to ignore his parents, to tune out their concerns and pleas" (105). What we see is the coming of age in his case; he wishes to come out of the shadow of his parents and yearns for his independent identity. So, "It is as Nikhil, that first semester, that he grows a goatee, starts smoking Camel Lights" (105). And yet it is not easy to dispense with his earlier identity as Gogol, particularly when his own parents address him as Nikhil in the company of his friends, keeping in mind his susceptibilities, but then he feels hurt as if he had been disowned by his parents.

Ruth Introduced

In the autumn of his sophomore year, he travels home by train and in the compartment he meets a girl named Ruth. It is discovered that both of them had studied the same subject, viz., Psychology at New Haven. He buys her tea and chips and takes coffee himself. They have an interesting conversation and after having taken their individual onward routes, get in touch on phone. Back at Yale the following week, they meet and get closer to each other. The meetings become regular. One day, she invites him to her room as her roommates are out for the day. It is here that Gogol has his first sexual experience with a girl.

Ruth had invited him to her home also and assured that he could stay there. But Gogol could not do that without telling his parents about Ruth. As things stand, "he has no patience for their surprise, their nervousness, their quiet disappointment, their questions about what Ruth's parents did and whether or not the relationship was serious" (115). He did not imagine her as his wife even though he continued meeting her. With the passage of time, his parents come to have a vague idea of Ruth. Gogol's sister Sonia also has a boyfriend about whom the parents are unaware. In fact, Sonia and Gogol have a kind of pact in keeping each other's affair secret. The parents told him one day that he was too young to get involved with a girl seriously. Gogol "pities his parents when they speak to him this way, for having no experience of being young and in love!" (117).

Ruth goes away to Oxford, England, to do her English major and Gogol feels very lonely. "It sickens him to think of the physical distance between them, to think that when he is asleep at night she is leaning over a sink somewhere, brushing her teeth and washing her face to start the next day. He longs for her as his parents have longed, all these years, for the people they love in India—for the first time in his life, he knows this feeling" (117). His only contact with her is through her letters.

There is mention of a panel discussion about Indian novels written in English which Gogol attends. He is informed by his mother about Amit, a distant cousin who is also a participant. The discussion centres round the identity problem of the ABCD—abbreviation for "American-born Confused Deshi." The term pejoratively sums up the condition of the second or later generation of Indians who migrated to America. The episode has been thrown in to give an ideational reference to the contemporary problem of identity.

Ruth stays on to complete a summer course at Oxford. Gogol is doing unpaid internship at a small architecture firm in Cambridge. He works at night washing dishes at an Italian restaurant to make some money. In this, he was following the general trend among the American youth who try to fend for themselves once they have graduated from school. Differences crop up between Gogol and Ruth and they start avoiding each other.

Naming Mystery Revealed

As he starts for his hometown in a train, the train stops at a station for a longer duration due to some accident and as a result, Gogol misses the commuter rail connection at Boston. When finally his train reaches the destination, he finds his father waiting anxiously in the cold at the station to receive him. As they drive home, his father tells him about the train accident involving himself way back in 1961 which he had so far kept a secret from his children. He did not remind himself of it because it was a near fatal accident. It was sheer anxiety at the delayed arrival of Gogol's train which made his father re-live that experience, the intensity of which forced him to blurt out the secret. He was seldom called Gogol now. He did not mind it since most of these three years, he has been addressed as Nikhil. Gogol feels angry at first at this revelation but then he realizes the emotional state of his father and feels repentant.

6. Gogol's Second Love

The year is 1994. After graduating as an architect from Columbia University, Gogol has taken up job with a firm in New York. His duty is to work with a team on designs for hotels, museums, corporate houses etc. He works late into evenings and gets paid quite handsomely. It is in New York that he gets involved with his second girlfriend Maxine or Max. As the intimacy between the two deepens, Gogol is drawn into Maxine's family also as she stays with her parents after her break-up with her previous boyfriend. Her house is replete with numerous artifacts and is aesthetically designed. As an architect Gogol feels interested in it.

He visits her formally when he is invited by her. At the dinner table, there is a genial atmosphere which strikes Gogol, for he has not been used to this kind of frankness in his own house when Bengali friends of his father visit it. Much to his surprise, Maxine's parents are least bothered about his visits to their daughter. He starts going to restaurants in her company. It becomes a routine with him to come back to her house after such forays. "Almost without fail they wind up back at her parents' place. There is always some delicious cheese or pate to snack on, always some good wine to drink" (136). He even stays overnight in her room and makes love to her. Surprisingly,

> Gerald and Lydia think nothing, in the mornings, when he and Maxine join them downstairs in the kitchen, their hair uncombed, seeking bowls of café au lait and toasted slices of French bread and jam. The first morning he'd slept over he'd been mortified to face them, showering before hand, putting on his wrinkled shirt and trousers from the day before, but they'd merely smiled, still in their bathrobes, and offered him warm sticky buns from their favourite neighborhood bakery and sections of the paper. (137)

It was just not possible for him to fall in love with Maxine without falling in love with "the house, and Gerald and Lydia's manner of living, for to know her and love her is to know and love all of these things" (137). He likes their lifestyle and moulds himself to be a part of this family. So, he helps them in the domestic chores as other Americans do. He also becomes habitual of seeing Maxine's parents curled up on the sofa in romantic mood. He is reminded of his parents whose physical relationship was too private an affair. It was, he recalls, "an utterly private, uncelebrated thing" (138).

His relationship with the Ratliffs deepens so much that within six months he gets the keys to the house, formally presented to him "on a silver Tiffany chain." He is as good as a member of the household and does the chores like taking the dog Silas out for walks and preparing for the weekend parties.

In June every year, both Gerald and Lydia go to their lake house in New Hampshire. Gerald's parents live there throughout the year. Their departure reminds Gogol of his own family's annual visits to Calcutta but there is a difference in that whereas the visits to India were paid as part of duty, here the Ratliffs visited New Hampshire only for the sake of pleasure.

After her parents have left, Maxine lives with Gogol. A strange feeling overtakes Gogol. He feels that he is not independent. "And yet for some reason, it is dependence, not adulthood, he feels. He feels free of expectation, of responsibility, in willing exile from his own life. He is responsible for nothing in the house; in spite of their absence, Gerald and Lydia continue to lord, however blindly, over their days. It is their books he reads, their music he listens to. Their front door he unlocks when he gets back from work. Their telephone messages he takes down" (142). Clearly, Gogol aspires to be the master of the house just as a mature person is expected to.

Lake-House Vacation

Their house here does not have air-conditioner, therefore it makes all the more sense that they move out to spend summer by the side of the lake in New Hampshire where it is much colder. Gogol does not wish to visit his own home, so he tells his parents that he is very busy with work because his firm is entering a competition for bagging work for a five-star hotel to be built in Miami. When his mother invites him to come over for the weekend, Gogol excuses himself saying he has to meet a deadline but actually he has to go to New Hampshire along with Maxine.

Gogol remembers vaguely that his father is to spend the following nine months with a colleague at a small university outside Cleveland, working on a project funded by his colleague's university. It was a prestigious grant the news of which was published in the newspapers also. Ashima had to stay back because Ashoke would be busy throughout the day at the lab. She wants him to see his father off but Gogol is least interested. He says that he has planned a vacation to New Hampshire. She says nothing but feels hurt to learn that her son would be vacationing with someone else's parents and not his own. On enquiring, she is told the name of the girl Gogol is seeing—Maxine.

However, on way to New Hampshire, Gogol and Maxine make a stopover at Pemberton Road for lunch "which is what he has agreed to" (145). He tells Maxine beforehand that they will not be able to touch or kiss each other in front of his parents and that there will be no wine with lunch. Maxine is amused. She sees Gogol's parents as "a single afternoon's challenge, an anomaly never to be repeated" (146). Obviously, Gogol is not able to view the lack of freedom in his family as a cultural difference vis-à-vis American families and is instead apologetic about it.

When they reach Gogol's home, his father is busy installing security system so that Ashima feels safe during his long absence. Maxine greets his parents by name as is the common practice in America. They are served sumptuous Indian lunch. His parents are not quite frank with Maxine even as they ask her sundry questions like which college she went to or what her parents did. After having lunch, Gogol leaves, promising to come back on the Thanksgiving Day. Maxine hears the word Gogol for the first time from the lips of his parents and wants to know about it, but Gogol promises to tell her about it later.

They reach the lake house. It is an old and musty house with primitive and mismatched furniture. The pipes in the bathroom are not covered. The floor does not run from wall to wall. There are unshaven logs supporting the roof. In short, it is just opposite of what they had in New York. To Maxine, however, "It's sort of like being at camp" (152). Maxine's grandparents—Hank and Edith live some houses away.

All day long, Gogol and Maxine walk about the house barefoot. Gogol goes for runs around the lake with Gerald. Gerald spends most of his time in his vegetable garden. One day, both

Gogol and Maxine swim over to their grandparents' house for lunch. At night, when the nights are rather warm, they go down to the lake, have a dip to cool themselves and after coming back to the shore make love also. There is practically nothing substantial to do. Gogol prepares a few sketches of the house. Slowly, he starts appreciating this idyllic place and its disconnect with the outside world but he is doubtful if his parents would like such a life. The periodic trips to Calcutta or even to strange places in America with his parents appear to Gogol "overwhelming, disorientating expeditions" (155).

> Yet he cannot picture his family occupying a house like this, playing board games on rainy afternoons, watching shooting stars at night, all their relatives gathered neatly on a small strip of sand. It is an impulse his parents have never felt, this need to be so far from things. They would have felt lonely in this setting, remarking that they were the only Indians. They would not want to go hiking, as he and Maxine and Gerald and Lydia do almost every day, up the rocky mountain trails, to watch the sun set over the valley. They would not care to cook with the fresh basil that grows rampant in Gerald's garden or to spend a whole day boiling blueberries for jam. His mother would not put on a bathing suit or swim. (155)

Maxine is told about the puzzle involving Gogol's first name. To her, it is "the cutest thing" she has ever heard. But she soon forgets about it. Gogol's twenty-seventh birthday is celebrated here. It is the first time that he is celebrating it away from his parents. Maxine and her mother prepare a special dinner after studying cookery books for days. Maxine's grandparents and a number of guests from the neighbourhood converge on the spot. He is introduced to others as the architect friend of Maxine. A couple is interested in building an addition to their cottage. Gogol promises to see them later. A woman comments about his being Indian to which Lydia responds saying that Nick (Nikhil) is American.

7. **Ashima Busies Herself**

This section begins with the description of Ashima preparing Christmas cards. A large number of cards have to be sent to the addresses noted in three address books which remind her of past. Normally she purchased greeting cards from the market but this year she is herself preparing them. She got the idea from a book she found in the crafts section of the library. Once a year, she has the chance to go through the pile of old greeting cards including the ones sent by her parents which usually make her cry. Since her husband is away to Cleveland to work on a research project for nine months and her children also stay at other places, she has all the time to do such things. The children are more of Americans now and they tell their mother, "Everyone should live on their own at some point" (161). But Ashima still does not like returning to an empty house after day's work at the library. Initially, she had been careful about checking the locks of doors before going to bed. She worked hard to keep the place tidy and things clean, but now she does not feel motivated to mind the dirt on things. How we relax in our private moments is meticulously noted by the author. For much of the upkeep of one's home, it seems the visits of the outsiders or even of one's near and dear ones are necessary.

> Now she does the laundry once a month. She no longer dusts, or notices dust, for that matter. She eats on the sofa, in single pot lasting her a week and an omlette to go with it if she has energy to bother. Sometimes she eats the way Gogol and Sonia do when they visit, standing in front of the refrigerator, not bothering to heat up the food in the oven or to put it on a plate. (162)

To keep herself a little busy, she continues to work three afternoons a week and two Saturdays a month at a public library. It is her first job in America. At first her duty was to put the books on shelves. Sometimes she cleans them with the help of a brush. She mends old books and arranges monthly displays on different subjects. There are other women workers also at the library with whom she has become friendly. Her husband comes home after three weeks. When he comes, she shops and cooks as she used to in the past. He pays all the bills and does strenuous jobs like raking the leaves on the lawn and putting gas in her car. This is typical Indian division of household labour. Like any Indian housewife, she too hands over her paychecks to her husband to be deposited in the bank.

Ashoke Passes Away

One afternoon, she gets a call from Ashoke informing her that he is in the hospital with stomach-ache. She is relieved to know that it is not a serious problem. He tells her that he drove to the hospital himself. Ashoke wants Ashima to fix an appointment with Dr. Sandler for the next Saturday so that he could get his full physical check-up done. She makes a note of it. She returns to prepare the Christmas cards again. This section also traces the stream of consciousness of Ashima who recalls past experiences as she writes the names of her children.

After sometime, she gets a phone call again from the hospital. This time it is the intern who had examined Ashoke, on the line. The female intern breaks the news of Ashoke's death to her. Ashima is not able to believe his word, for Ashoke had complained of stomach-ache only. So, she wants the intern to check if there is a mistake of some sort, but the lady at the other end tells her that he had a severe heart attack and that all attempts to revive him failed. Ashima's state of mind, at this point, has been graphically captured by the writer and underlines the irrationality into which the shocking news sends her:

> Instead of answering, Ashima hangs up the phone as the woman is still speaking, pressing down the receiver as hard as she can into the cradle, keeping her hand there for a full minute, as if to smother the words she's just heard. She stares at her empty teacup, and then at the kettle on the stove, which she'd had to turn off in order to hear her husband's voice just a few hours ago. She begins to shiver violently, the house instantly feeling twenty degrees colder. She pulls her sari tightly around her shoulders, like a shawl. She gets up and walks systematically through the rooms of the house, turning on all the light switches, turning on the lamppost on the lawn and floodlight over the garage, as if she and Ashoke are expecting company. [. . .] She opens her address book, suddenly unable to remember her son's phone number, a thing she can normally dial in her sleep. (169)

Finally, she does telephone her children. Sonia flies in from San Francisco to be with her. Gogol reaches Cleveland to get the body of his father. It was the night before that Gogol and Maxine had gone to a book party and later to dinner with a small group. When he returned, he was told by Maxine's parents that his mother had called twice. As he turned to leave with his arm around Maxine's waist, the phone rang again. This time it was Sonia on the line who finally delivered him the sad news.

Gogol reaches the hospital in Cleveland where his father's body was kept in the morgue. So far his state of mind is seen to be normal. He notes the absence of any magazines in the waiting room and even feels hungry at the sight of the food cart in the lift. Finally, he is shown the body of his father lying in the morgue. The face is yellow and bloated and the lips colourless. He identifies the body for the hospital record. He is handed over the personal belongings of his father including the wallet and car keys. He tells the hospital authorities that at his father's funeral no religious services are required. They tell him that he could pick up his father's ashes along with the death certificate after a few days or these could be sent by them to the Pemberton Road address.

Gogol leaves for the apartment at Baron's Court where his father had been staying for the past three months. He notes the similarity of buildings here which upsets his architect's mind. The reality of his father's death overtakes him at this point: "Thinking of his father living here alone these past three months, he feels the first threat of tears, but he knows that his father did not mind, that he was not offended by such things" (174).

Reaching the apartment, he is lost in memories of his father. He had been told by his mother not to bring back anything from the apartment. Therefore, he had to dispose of the things lying here. The pieces of furniture brought on rental had to be returned. Useful items had to be dumped in the basement of the apartment block so that those interested in making use of them could take them. It is the usual practice in America. He feels guilty of throwing away food items because his father never wasted anything. The useless items had to be put into garbage bags. He informs the University office of his father's death and also asks for the cancellation of utilities like electricity and gas supplies. Much against Maxine's advice, he spends the night in the apartment. Next morning at ten, he gets up and catches flight for Boston where his mother and sister along with some friends of the family will be waiting for him. He is afraid of seeing his mother in such a situation.

Ashima is not alone now. Sonia and Gogol are with her. For the first week, friends keep pouring in. There are many who call her from different parts of America. The post-death rituals observed by the traditional Hindùs have been described minutely by the novelist. They take simple food for these ten days and stay, for the first time, as a family. At the end of the mourning period, they invite friends in America to a religious ceremony. After this, Ashima gets busy with the formalities like change of name in bank account, mortgage agreement, bills of all types etc. She does not wish to go to Calcutta but wants to stay in the house where her husband breathed his last. Gogol goes back to New York to carry on with his work. The chapter concludes with the recollection of Gogol's memories of his father. He remembers having visited a lighthouse at Cape Cod where they reached the tip of the piece of land jutting into the sea and could go no farther. "Don't go too far," his mother had warned, "don't go so that I can't see you" (185). They had forgotten to bring their camera but his father had said, "Remember that you and I made this journey, that we went together to a place where there was nowhere left to go" (187).

8. Maxine Parts Company

This chapter takes up the thread of the plot after a year. Gogol has rented an apartment on Amsterdam Avenue. He is working for his old firm. Maxine continued to live with him for sometime but gradually she lost patience as Gogol would be silent at the dinner table and rather indifferent in bed. He was now more concerned about his mother and sister with whom he would converse telephonically every evening. He would go over to see them every weekend. He did not take her along, nor was she invited to go to Calcutta with the rest of the family. In this, Gogol was being too private and Maxine was being treated as an outsider even though she desired to be part of the family. The shock following his father's death had bereft him of his love for Maxine. Instead of analyzing his behaviour towards Maxine, Gogol walked out on her one day for good. Later, she got engaged to another person.

Gogol continues to visit his mother on weekends. His mother has become thinner and her hair has started greying. He is preparing for his registration exam so that he can practise architecture independently. He joins a class for the purpose where he meets Bridget, an attractive woman with short brown hair. She is married and on weekends, she sees her husband who works as a professor in Boston. He loves his wife so much that he has insisted on having her name on the mail box and her voice on the answering machine. In this way, he derives solace in her absence. However, in New York, Gogol takes her to his apartment and engages in sex with her. When the thought of her loving husband comes to his mind, he feels guilty.

Moushumi Introduced

His mother is concerned about Gogol's love life. She enquires whether he has a new girl-friend or if it is possible for him to patch up with Maxine. One day, his mother asks him to call up Moushumi, the daughter of the Mazoomdar couple who, like Gogol's parents belong to India but are settled in the U.S.A. Gogol had known her as a teenager. His earliest recollection of her was at a party in his house where she was asked to go and watch the television with other children and her response was: "I detest American television." Her British accent had become a matter of joke among the youngsters gathered there. He remembered calling her mother 'Rina Mashi.' His mother tells him that Moushumi has had a break-up before marriage. In order to humour his mother, he agrees to see her.

They meet at a bar and develop intimacy. She is a studious type and always carries a book along to read during free time. Even when Gogol reaches the bar to meet her, she is lost in a book. Although it was a blind date engineered by their mothers, they develop a liking for each other. They talk about so many things—Gogol's bereavement, the house in which his mother lives, Moushumi's life in New York etc. She can recollect minutely the details of the house which she had visited as a teenager. She is a candidate for Ph.D. in French literature at the NYU (New York University). She has been living in New York for the past two years, supporting herself with mofussil jobs. She stayed in Paris also but came to New York for the sake of her lover who later ditched her. Gogol also remembers that she ignored him at his graduation party at which she was a guest.

After drinks at the bar and dinner at a French restaurant and before taking leave of her, he asks, "Should we make our parents happy and see each other again?" to which she replies a non-committal "Maybe" and later more purposive "Give me a call" (198). Later, he tries to analyze in his mind as to what had attracted him towards her and feels that it was the familiarity that made him curious to know more about her. In the days that follow, he continues to think of her. His infatuation for Moushumi is evident from the following description: "He struggles but fails to recall her presence at Pemberton road; still, he is secretly pleased that she has seen those rooms, tasted his mother's cooking, washed her hands in the bathroom, however long ago" (200).

They meet after a week at an Italian restaurant for lunch. When she tells him that she had taught students that day, he feels jealous of students who had the opportunity to watch a beautiful teacher three times a week. There are more memories to share with each other. Since the weather is getting colder and Gogol has not cared to dress up properly for it, she offers him her scarf. Gogol declines it but he is "half tempted to say yes, to feel her scarf against his skin" (204). They visit a boutique, where she buys a cap for him. While making payment for it, she takes fancy to a velvet hat and tries it on her head. As she puts it on, a customer compliments her, but the price is high and so she does not buy it. Gogol, however, returns later when she is gone, buys it and keeps it at his apartment waiting to present it to her on her birthday.

The next weekend, Moushumi invites Gogol to her place for dinner. Gogol takes along with him a bunch of sunflowers and a bottle of wine. He helps her in the kitchen where she is frying some big pieces of chicken. She needs to take off her specs and Gogol helps her in the act but the casual touch with her body arouses him sensually and after that it is a short walk from the kitchen to the bedroom. The intimacy deepens and within six months "they have clothes and toothbrushes at each other's apartments" (211). They have a lot in common to talk about, as for example, the frequent trips to Calcutta in the company of their respective parents. Both of them faced the peculiar problem in America when they were assumed to be Greek, Egyptian or Mexican nationals because of their brownish colour. It may be added here that the wheatish colour and the features of the North Indians resemble those of the people belonging to the Caribbean and South American countries among others.

Moushumi's Past

Moushumi reveals her past love life to Gogol. Whereas during her college days, she had not dared to strike relationship in reality with anyone, she rather repented after she passed out of college. After moving to Paris, she put down all her defences and allowed herself to be won over by men of different nationalities and ages. There were Germans, Persians, Italians among them but most of all these were French. Even in the span of a day, she slept with one man after lunch, another after dinner. "They were a bit excessive" she told Gogol. (215)

Her job in Paris was to help American businessmen learn French and this came in handy to strike relationships with them. Finally, she fell in love with Graham, an investment banker from New York who was living in Paris. For his sake, she joined the New York University. Both of them lived in New York, without letting their families know. When her parents came to visit her, he would disappear to a hotel "removing all traces of himself from the apartment" (216). Later, she introduced him to her parents who did not raise any objection because most of the other Bengali girls of her age in their friends' circle had been married off. Before marriage, Graham flew into Calcutta to meet the large number of Moushumi's relatives. Back in New Jersey, however, he was heard complaining in a merry company about his stay in Calcutta. He found the Indian culture "repressing" and the society "somewhat provincial" (217). "Imagine dealing with fifty in-laws without alcohol," he commented. Moushumi realized that he had been fooling everybody. They argued and differences cropped up between them. In a moment of rage, she took off the engagement ring and threw it into the street. Subsequently, Graham moved out of her apartment and her life.

9. An Indian Wedding

Within a year, Gogol and Moushumi get married in typical Bengali style in New Jersey. The chapter contains details of preparations for the marriage. An hour-long ceremony takes place in a hotel where the management does not allow them to light the holy fire. After the ceremony, the reception takes place for which both of them change clothes. Many people attend the function and congratulate the newly-wed. A cake is cut on the occasion. Everybody is relaxed for both of them are Bengalis and as such they are fulfilling a deep-seated desire of their parents and community.

The honeymoon is postponed for the present because Moushumi has to teach a class three days after her wedding. He presents her the hat she had liked at a store quite sometime back. Naturally, she feels overwhelmed. The chapter details the intimate moments of the newly-weds at the Double Tree hotel. Afterwards, they total up the gift cheques which comes to $ 7,035. Moushumi would not change her name to Moushumi Ganguli after the marriage. They rent a one-bedroom apartment off the Third Avenue in New York. A few weekends have to be spent in equipping the house with furniture and furnishings. They throw parties on occasions for their friends—architects at Gogol's firm and Moushumi's student friends at the NYU.

The French Sojourn

In March, they go to Paris where Moushumi is to read a paper at a conference at the University of Sorbonne. They stay at an apartment owned by a male friend of Moushumi. Gogol tries to keep himself busy with visits to places of architectural interest but on the whole, he feels himself useless here. One reason is also Moushumi's felicity with the French language as opposed to Gogol's ignorance. His condition is described graphically by the writer, "Part of him knows this is a privilege, to be here with a person who knows the city so well, but the other part of him wants simply to be a tourist, fumbling with a phrase book, looking at all the buildings on his list, getting lost" (231). She tries to help him with a few phrases in French and guides him about the city. On their last day, he shops for gifts for his relatives. It emerges that she is sad to be leaving Paris.

The Name-Game and Disillusionment

The parties become a routine: "But this is life now, the weekend sometimes more tiring than the workweek, an endless stream of dinner parties, cocktail parties, occasional after-eleven parties with dancing and drugs to remind them that they are still young, followed by Sunday brunches full of unlimited Bloody Marys and over-priced eggs" (236). One such party at Brooklyn in the house of Donald and Astrid, who are Moushumi's friends, has been described in detail. It was through this couple that Moushumi had met Graham, her former fiancé. They are all married and some of them are known to Gogol but he is not interested in the tête-à-tête. These days, the small talk at these parties inclines towards names of newborn children because some woman is found to be in family way. By chance, on this night, they start discussing names. Moushumi's name is explained as a "damp southwesterly breeze" (240). It is revealed at this point by Moushumi that Nikhil had changed his name. This surprises all present and they become quiet. Gogol had not expected her to blurt out the secret. "He stares at her, stunned. He has never told her not to tell anyone. He simply assumed she never would. His expression is lost on her; she smiles back at him, unaware of what she's done. The dinner guests regard him, their mouths hanging open in confused smiles" (243). This episode inevitably leads to his former name Gogol and even though another guest

Sally can place the name as belonging to the writer of the short story 'Overcoat,' others including Donald consider it a queer name.

Gogol slowly gets disillusioned with Moushumi. The scent of her body which intoxicated him seems now suppressed by the stale smell of smoke left behind by her excessive smoking:

> These days, the stale smell of it, in her hair and on her fingertips, and in the bedroom where she sits typing, slightly disgusts him, and from time to time he can't help but have a fleeting vision of himself, tragically abandoned as a result of her mild but persistent addiction. When he'd admitted his fear to her one day, she'd laughed. "Oh, Nikhil," she'd said, "you can't be serious." (237)

10. The Moody Intellectual

On their first wedding anniversary, Moushumi has her joy tripled as she has successfully passed her oral exam and she has been awarded a research scholarship to work on her dissertation in France for one year but she decides not to avail of it. She seems to be rather seriously concerned about the responsibilities of her married life, but finally it is her impulses that outweigh her mental calculations. On the pretext of studying, she has been indulging in innocent activities of her choice like going for a walk by herself or seeing Astrid and her baby. She wants to reassure herself that she could still be independent. What she understands by personal freedom is laxity in sexual matters—something linked to basic instincts. This can be called skewed understanding only but this is what dominates her character.

They dress up appropriately for the anniversary—Nikhil putting on the moss-coloured shirt presented by Moushumi and she the pashmina shawl gifted by him. At the restaurant, she asks him if he remembers the black dress she is wearing. It is the one that she wore when they met the first time and later when they slept together but Nikhil fails to recall and this disappoints her. However, she is not surprised because she knows he is a busy architect now. Finally, after some search, they land up at the restaurant of their choice. The air conditioner has lowered the temperature within and Moushumi feels very cold. This apart, the waiter who attends on her does not look into their eyes. All of a sudden, she has an urge to leave the place. She had done precisely this on an earlier occasion in a hair salon when she felt the behaviour of the stylist insulting. At this moment, she also feels she is not quite merry even after consuming two cocktails and a bottle of wine which she shared with Nikhil. They finally leave the restaurant and since Moushumi is still hungry, she suggests entering a pizza eatery.

Dimitri: A Wish Fulfilled

Moushumi's eighth semester has begun at the NYU. One fine morning, she gets ready to go to the university even though Nikhil is yet asleep. But when she reaches her workplace, she finds people crowding around a dead body which is found to be of Alice, an administrative assistant. She feels sick as it reminds her of the death of Nikhil's father. When she goes to check her mailbox, she finds an envelope sent by Dimitri Desjardins to a professor. The name sends her down the memory lane. She opens the envelope and finds a covering letter and a resume.

She remembers having met this man years ago at a rally held in Washington D.C. during her final months of high school. While journeying back by bus, she was with him in the bus. He flirted with her briefly in a state of half-sleep but when he woke up, he held back from kissing Moushumi even though she was ready for it. He had only said, "You're going to break hearts, you know" (259). She met him again at the university, had coffee with him and when she asked him to be her date at a school programme, he declined though he drove her home and also kissed her lightly. Later, she saw him with his date, a tall freckled girl. He told her that he was going to Europe, ostensibly in the company of that girl. They kept in touch with each other through letters for sometime. His last communication had contained a box of books.

Back at home, she locates a novel titled *The Red and the Black* which bears dedication "To Mouse" (her pet name given by Dimitri) and is signed "Love Dimitri" (261). She also recovers an envelope containing some postcards mailed by him to her.

Next week, she calls up Dimitri. They begin meeting every Monday and Wednesday and as is wont with Moushumi, the meeting routine starts with lunch at Dimitri's apartment and ends in his bedroom. For the first month, Nikhil does not notice her absence. She starts meeting Dimitri on Fridays as well. But Gogol does not suspect anything.

11.

Gogol is alone at home as Moushumi is away to Palm Beach attending a conference. We are told of Sonia and Ashima's visit to Gogol's apartment last week on the occasion of Thanksgiving. It was the first time he had not gone either to his parents' or to his in-laws' house for a holiday. Sonia's husband Ben had also come along. All of them celebrate together. The question comes to his mind if he was making Moushumi happy. As it is, they did not argue, still had sex and she did not accuse him but "more and more he sensed distance, her dissatisfaction, her distraction" (272). He thinks a trip to a place which none of them had seen before would set the matters right.

12. The Journey Continues

This is the concluding chapter. The year is 2000 A.D. Ashima is preparing for a party. She will be leaving Pemberton Road house where she has lived for twenty-seven years. The house has been sold recently. She intends spending six months in India and the remaining six months in the U.S.A. She would be truly "without borders"—true to the meaning of her name "Ashima." She has an American passport now. She lights an incense and takes it to different rooms, stopping awhile in front of Ashoke's image. Each one of her jobs connected with today's final celebratory meal for her children is special. While standing in front of the mirror in the bathroom, she remembers that she is a fifty-three year old widow now. She had come as a new bride here. In between, she played the role of a wife. Perhaps, she would be a grandmother also. Then she would arrive in America "laden with hand-knit sweaters and gifts" something which her grandmother had done. Life seems to have completed its circular course.

When Gogol gets off the train, there is nobody to receive him; therefore he sits down on a bench. He has come with the intent to help his mother pack her things and settle her accounts before he sees her off at the airport. Now that the moment of separation from his mother has come, his dormant feelings are aroused. As he analyzes his attitude towards his parents vis-à-vis their attitude toward their own parents back in Calcutta, Gogol now appreciates their several trips to Calcutta.

He also recalls his break-up with Moushumi a year ago. They were going to spend Christmas with his mother and Sonia. Moushumi favoured renting a house in Siena along with Donald and Astrid but Gogol was not in favour of it. At that moment, she had blurted out, "Dimitri says Siena is something out of a fairy tale" (282). What happened was really dramatic: "Immediately, a hand had gone to her mouth, accompanied by a small intake of breath. And then, silence. 'Who's Dimitri?' he'd asked. And then: 'Are you having an affair?' [. . .] But as soon as he asked it, he knew" (282). The answer was not given but was rightly taken as "Yes." He felt sick that night. He did not tell his mother but suffered silently. However, she told him the whole story and "for the first time, another man's name upset Gogol more than his own" (283). The day after Christmas, she left Pemberton Road on the pretext of some interview. When he reached back, he found her belongings missing from the apartment. She had left for ever. Later, she did meet him in his office to get the divorce papers signed.

Sonia and Ben arrive to take Gogol home. She is working as an attorney now but while welcoming home, she speaks the way she did as a child: "Welcome home, Goggles," she says. (284). They decorate the old artificial Christmas tree. They tease Sonia reminding her of her college days when she had taken a class in Hinduism and thereafter refused to receive the Christmas gifts saying they were not Christians. Except for the rituals concerning marriage and death, this is the only reference to religion as an issue in the novel. The guests start pouring in at seven-thirty and the party starts. They recall the Christmas celebrations held earlier in the Pemberton Road house when Ashoke was alive. Now they would miss these parties. Ashima asks Gogol to bring the camera and get some photographs. He goes upstairs to get his father's Nikon camera. There are so many things lying there, out of which he picks up a book—*The Short Stories of Nikolai Gogol*—which had been presented to him on his birthday by his father. It still bears the inscription: "For Gogol Ganguli" and alongside are the words in his father's hand: "The man who gave you his name, from the man who gave you your name" (288). His father's handwriting reminds him of the cheques that his father used to send him throughout his career as a college student. Gogol realizes that after his mother is gone, the name Gogol Ganguli would vanish from the lips of his loved ones and so, "cease to exist" (289). This is disconcerting rather than reassuring for him.

Gogol now compares the life of Nikolai Gogol with his own. After a month, he would be starting on a new job producing his own designs and it is very likely that he would become an associate of the firm and his name Nikhil would be incorporated in the firm's name. Thus, whereas the name Gogol was purposely hidden, Nikhil would live on. He starts reading the first story. The rest of the story contained in the final one page or so of the novel is noted in future tense: "In a few minutes his mother will come upstairs to find him. 'Gogol,' she will say, opening the door without knocking, 'where is the camera? What's taking so long? This is no time for books,' she will scold, hastily noting the volume open" (290). The writer says Gogol will apologize and go down with his mother and be witness to what had usually been the party scene when his father was alive.

While the discontinuation of the present tense narrative indicates end of the story, the shift to the future tense indicates continuation of life along the pattern hinted at. For the present, Gogol is happy to have recovered the book which would otherwise have been lost. He continues reading the book while his mother is busy downstairs not knowing what her son is doing.

Chapter 4

Major Themes in *The Namesake*

The Namesake can be primarily viewed as a diasporic text to which the sub-themes of family ties, clash of values, cross-cultural relationships, love and loneliness etc. contribute. At the deeper level, "*The Namesake* is a story of guilt and liberation; in this sense, it speaks to the universal struggle to extricate ourselves from the past—from family and obligation and the curse of history" (Hallgren). It is a deeply moving and finely wrought family drama that takes up Jhumpa Lahiri's favourite subject of immigrant experience. Here is the Ganguli couple, the first generation Indian immigrants whose experiences in the U.S. are pitted against those of their children, complicated further by the choice of name for their son, all of which leads to the clash of cultures and tangled ties between generations. Before delving deep into the thematic aspects further, let us ponder over the meaning and origin of the term 'diaspora.'

The origin of the word 'diaspora' is from the Greek *dia* (= through) and *speirein* (= to scatter). As such, it gives the sense of dispersal through space. Its use in the context of the Jewish community, which was without a state of its own, was quite justified. The Jews had been stateless since Biblical times and were spread all over the world, where they faced discrimination and oppression. The term 'Diaspora' referred to these Jews. It was only in 1949 that the present state of Israel was carved out of the Palestine territory occupied by the Allied powers during the Second World War. This creation of the new nation has not been peaceful and even now it continues to be a major cause of conflict in the Arab region.

However, the term became popular and was used in the context of other nationalities also which had been displaced from the original homelands due to one reason or the other. Not going far back in time, we can relate the present major diasporas to the period when certain nations of Europe became maritime powers and started the phase of colonization which led to the system of slavery whereby human beings were forcibly captured and made to work like cattle in distant colonies. The black population of America owes its origin to this inhuman practice.

When slavery was abolished by the British government in 1833-34, France and Holland also followed suit. In its place, the system of indentured labour was introduced and large contingents of people were taken from colonies by the colonizers to other places where they were treated as bonded labourers. It happened in the case of Indians who were taken to far-off Mauritius, Fiji or South Africa by the ruling British to work as plantation workers. Other colonial powers like France and Portugal also took Indian workers to Surinam, Martinique, Angola, Mozambique etc. Similarly, Indian soldiers were forcibly sent by the British rulers to fight wars on their behalf.

The second wave of immigration was not under duress. Business-minded Gujarati people moved to certain African countries like Kenya and South Africa for the sake of establishing business there and created what is dubbed as the 'trade diaspora.' More recent times saw the migration of skilled and semi-skilled manpower, mainly from Kerala, to the oil-rich Sheikhdoms of the United Arab Emirates. Also professionals and entrepreneurs went to the First World countries like UK and USA. After a gap, this trend has picked up in our times as the third wave of migration of professionals and educated elite who have gone wherever they could find greener pastures.

Even though distinction has to be made between forced and willing movement of people, the phenomenon of diaspora necessarily involves a "structure of location followed by dislocation and relocation" (Paranjape 59). Moving away from one's homeland and settling elsewhere on long-term basis does mean dislocation that brings in a sense of loss and nostalgia. This is followed by a bid for relocation in an alien milieu through negotiation and adjustment. And yet there is no guarantee that the outcome will be sure success; hybridity or in-betweenness being quite common here.

All such Indians who have been living outside India constitute the Indian diaspora. The Indian diaspora, which is twenty million strong and is scattered in more than 110 countries of the world (Sharma 19), has never stopped looking back at their homeland. When India was under the British rule, the diaspora shaped the history of the independence movement of India. In the post-independence scenario, it has contributed to the raising of foreign currency reserves through remittances and in this they have achieved top position among all the diasporas of the world. They have also invested in economic and social uplift of the country. Of course, there is also the lunatic fringe that has been instrumental in instigating subversive movements in India but then a little chaff always comes with the grain.

Diasporic Traits

According to John Hartley, diasporic communities are groups of people that are distanced from their homeland—as political or economic migrants in search of work or refugees escaping war. The experience of exile may be accompanied by a sense of belonging to the former homeland and a continued allegiance to that remembered culture while staying within the host country. As such, the diasporas can be defined as "heterogeneous cultures, spatially separated from their place of origin yet living between places in their identity and cultural life" (66). The stress on in-betweenness in such cases has to be underlined here. This very characteristic has been brashly put forth by Salman Rushdie in his *Imaginary Homelands*: "Sometimes we feel that we straddle two cultures; at other times, that we fall between two stools" (15).

Pointing to the common characteristics of the diaspora members, William Safren (qtd. Satendra Nandan, 53) comments that they "retain a collective memory, vision or myth about their original homeland" and believe they cannot be fully accepted by their lost society and therefore feel partly alienated. At the same time, they "regard their ancestral homeland as their true, ideal home and as the place to which they or their descendents would (or should) eventually return when conditions are appropriate." They continue to relate to that homeland and also feel committed to its maintenance or restoration. As can be seen, these characteristics are not without gaps and contradictions which is a concomitant of the essentializing process that overlooks the differences in which the diaspora members live.

The descendants of the diasporic people develop their own culture which is built on their original form but understandably, involves a lot of inter-mingling with the culture of the host country. According to Bill Ashcroft, "The development of diasporic cultures necessarily questions essentialist models, interrogating the ideology of a unified, 'natural' cultural norm, one that underpins the centre/margin model of colonialist discourse" (70).

It is common experience that when one, driven away from home due to economic compulsions / ambitions, has been living abroad for a long time, one feels homesick. This is on two counts: one misses the extended family and friends back home. The time spent in the country of origin is the early part of life—childhood, adolescence etc. when experience of life under the care of parents is positive and enjoyable. Secondly, lack of proper adjustment within the milieu of the adopted country at a stage in life when struggle is called for, makes one turn to pleasant memories of the native land. In such a situation, the bonding of culture, religion, literature and language is especially strong among the expatriates. But whereas it provides ethnic identity and a sense of self, it can also alienate one from the host culture. It is this displacement which gives diasporic writing its peculiar sense of loss and nostalgia. Therefore, loss and nostalgia constitute key elements of any diasporic writing. At the same time, it gives vent to a certain alienation due to incomplete assimilation in the adopted society.

Another way to look at the diasporic writing is to note the motifs of dislocation, homelessness, rootlessness and escape. John Hartley rightly states: "The psychological and cultural experience of diaspora can be one of hybridity, exile, nostalgia, selective adaptation or cultural invention" (66). It is this experience that is sought to be transmitted to readers through the diasporic literature. The diaspora writers are obsessed with search for identity and their writing displays a poetics of exile and displacement.

So far as the writers of the Indian diaspora are concerned, from Raja Rao and G.V. Desani to Jhumpa Lahiri and Arvind Adiga, a number of them have tried to give expression to their experiences and reflections. One can simply not miss out on Salman Rushdie, Vikram Seth, V.S. Naipaul, Bharati Mukherjee, Rohinton Mistry, M.G. Vassanji, Amitav Ghosh, Homi Bhabha, Gayatri Spivak, Firdaus Kanga, Boman Desai, Kiran Desai, Ardashir Vakil et al.

Jhumpa Lahiri, herself a second-generation child of Indian immigrants in the USA, occupies what Homi Bhabha refers to as the "interstitial" position and is eminently qualified to represent the immigrant Indian in American society. She was born in England of Bengali parents. Her father made USA his home in 1969 at the age of forty, prior to which he was resident in India. Talking about her childhood, Jhumpa says, "There were invisible walls erected around our home, walls intended to keep American influence at bay. Growing up I was admonished not to 'behave like an American' or worse to 'think' of myself as one" (Patil 145). Her in-betweenness, so very characteristic of the diasporic, is also reflected in another comment that she makes with regard to visits to Calcutta which she undertook along with her parents: "I belonged there in some fundamental way, in a way; I didn't seem to belong in the US" (*ibid*). This places her almost in the category of the ABCD or the 'American born confused Desi'—a class that is discussed in one of the scenes in her novel.

Jhumpa Lahiri knows the American landscape and the mindscape like the back of her hand. She also knows well the community of expatriate Bengalis in the Boston area; their peculiarly lonely lives punctuated by periodic get-togethers of fellow expatriates; the customs and worldview through which they see their own everyday experience; and the struggle of their American children with their own questions of identity and belonging. Her work has primarily focused on first and second-generation Bengali immigrants, exploring themes of exile, isolation, and assimilation. Lahiri's insight into the psychology of relationships, aging, maturity, and loss is remarkable. Her subject, in the novel as also in her stories, is the loneliness of dislocation. What makes her work stand out is, at least, partly due to the gentle and persuasive way in which the atmosphere of displacement is evoked. In the present novel, she talks about Gogol, a young man about the same age as the author, born like her to immigrant parents from West Bengal, who grows up into a brilliant student and a successful architect even as he has to struggle to discover himself through successive ill-fated relationships and appreciate the worth of expectations of his parents.

Identity Problem

The problem of identity is writ large all over diasporic fiction. The fact that Jhumpa Lahiri has chosen *The Namesake* as the title of the novel shows the importance that she attaches to the identity of her protagonist. The naming of the lead character as Gogol and later as Nikhil brings in a conflict between both names and the identities attached to them. 'Gogol' is a Russian name and seems irrelevant to the boy as it is neither American nor Indian. He has hard time explaining it to his friends and others as to why such a name was given him in the first place. In a way, the problem regarding the name symbolizes the problem of his identity: who exactly is he—American or Indian or someone else? In the precarious situation in which he is placed—son of Indian immigrant family brought up in America and torn between opposite pulls of his peers and parents—he fails to understand whether he should listen to his mind or his heart until his father's death tilts the balance on one side.

The postcolonial discourse attaches great importance to the question of identity. First underlined in the context of newly-free nations, the notion was quickly taken up to describe the condition of any minority group pitted against a majority based on different colour, race, sex etc. In the case of the immigrants in any society, their identity is threatened by the culture of the host country. The trajectory of a migrant follows the pattern of location, dislocation and relocation, each one of these phases being liminal rather than sharply defined ones. The process of acculturation is a slow one-sided (the minority seeking integration with the majority) one and is not without a sense of loss and exile. It is also not clear transformation; it gives rise to hybridity marking different stages of acculturation. According to Homi Bhabha, "This interstitial passage between fixed identifications opens up the possibility of a cultural hybridity that entertains difference without an assumed or imposed hierarchy" (4).

Through her masterly art, Lahiri gives different dimensions to what a name can mean. It is not only the way others know you but also how you view yourself. She underlines the efforts required to mediate between people and situations as also between cultures and social practices. According to Julie Myerson of the *Guardian,* "This is a novel that explores the concepts of cultural identity, of rootlessness, of tradition and familial expectation but never succumbs to the clichés those themes so often entail. Instead, Lahiri turns it into something both larger and simpler: the story of a man and his family, of his life and hopes, woes and sorrows." There are, therefore, no lengthy articulations of what constitutes diasporic condition.

For the Indian parents, the children are known by their special names given for the purpose. We may call them nick names but these are not the fixed nick names the like of which Americans use, as for example, every William will be called Bill and every Elizabeth, Lizzy. So far as the Indian parents are concerned, "No parent ever called a child by his good name. Good names had no place within a family" (165). The good names are the ones used publicly and their need arises when the child enters a school. In Gogol's case too, the parents wanted to change the name to Nikhil and had filled the form in his first school for this purpose, but then Gogol had not been prepared beforehand for this change. As a result, he failed to respond to questions put to him when the Principal addressed him as Nikhil. Sensing the child's inclination for it, she changed the name to Gogol. This very liking for the name changes into hatred when Gogol's classmates make fun of his name. Sometimes they would pester him, corrupting his name to "Giggle" or "Gargle" (65).

That Gogol, as a child, was aware of the importance of identity is revealed by the field visit of his class to the graveyard where other children located the graves of the members of their clan as revealed by the surname mentioned in the epitaph, but to his dismay, he could not find any 'Ganguli' buried there (91). His first name 'Gogol' did not relate him to either the Indian community or the American and so it dampened his spirits. When his teacher taught Nikolai Gogol to the class, Gogol Ganguli squirmed and winced, for Mr. Lawson used certain unpleasant phrases in giving biographical details like 'eccentric genius,' 'queer and sickly creature,' 'deeply paranoid, frustrated man,' 'morbidly melancholic' etc. (91).

It was only in 1986, when he entered Yale as a freshman that Gogol changed his name to "Nikhil" but it created a different kind of psychological problem for him. As the writer points out, he did not yet feel like Nikhil. So, "after eighteen years of Gogol, two months of Nikhil feel scant, inconsequential. At times he feels as if he's cast himself in a play acting the part of twins, indistinguishable to the naked eye yet fundamentally different."(105) The loss of the old name is not so easy to forget, as for example, when his parents try to contact him on phone and have to speak to his roommates. They refer to their son as 'Gogol.' At such moments, he feels as if he is not their child. "Gogol feels helpless, annoyed yet unable to blame his mother, caught in the mess he's made" (106). When on alternate weekends, he visits home, "Somewhere along the two-and-a-half-hour journey, Nikhil evaporates and Gogol claims him again." (106). Thus, he tried to correct the randomness and irrelevance of the name, but he could not free himself from this bondage and "reinvent himself fully."

The name-change was sought to be relegated to past but its ghost got up once when he visited home in Maxine's company and his father addressed him as "Gogol." The writer herself refers to him as Gogol. He had learnt, by now, from his father the secret of his christening—the story of the train accident and of Nikolai Gogol's story book. He appreciated the importance of the name for it symbolized a new life for his father. His father did not want to tell him because it reminded him of that nightmare. Later, when his wife Moushumi blurted out the secret, he felt cheated and hurt.

Towards the end of the novel, we find that Gogol grows philosophical. His marriage was a failure and then his father's death was the worst accident. We find that Gogol has re-connected himself with the family and drawn the right inspiration from his father's life. At thirty-two, he is now mature enough to appreciate fully what his parents went through—how they lived a lonely life, away from their near and dear ones for so long. One has to move on in life. The house in which he and Sonia grew up will be lost to them. He is ready to launch his own firm in the land of promise and build the goodwill of his own name, even as he rues the loss of his old name due to dispersal of family.

Immigrant Experience

The diasporic fiction tries to capture the sense of displacement of the diasporic. It provides immigrants' perception of the new homeland against the backdrop of his memory of the lost homeland. Loss and nostalgia are, therefore, key characteristics of diasporic writing. To start with, we are led into the field of experience not of Ashoke but of Ashima who arrives in America as his newly-wed wife. The first shock in store for her is the chilly weather. She is uninitiated into the ways of American society. By and by, she gets used to things here. After her husband gives her directions in this regard, she learns to go out independently to nearby departmental stores to do shopping.

When a new immigrant gets settled in a foreign land, she compares things in the host country with the ones in her home country. As Ashima is admitted to the hospital for delivery, time sits heavy on her heart, but no, it is *American time* now: "American seconds tick on top of her pulse point. For half a minute, a band of pain wraps around her stomach. [. . .] She calculates the

Indian time on her hands" (4). Ashima feels lonely even though there are three other pregnant women—all Americans in the same room, separated by curtains. She is aware of the concern for privacy of Americans. "But she has gathered that Americans, in spite of their public declarations of affection, in spite of their miniskirts and bikinis, in spite of their hand-holding on the street and lying on top of each other on the Cambridge Common, prefer their privacy" (3).

She learns about the American lifestyle, like people do not take off shoes before entering house. Even trays of cat litter could be seen in the kitchen. (51) Ashima is aghast to learn that Gogol was taken along with other class-mates to a graveyard and asked to trace on paper the names etched on gravestones. (70) Besides, the attempt to fill up the void in life with material things is also noted by Lahiri, as Hallgren points out: "Absent proper kinship ties, she seems to be saying, this is how Americans feel most at home: among their things. Refined as it may be, consumerism has touched these characters to the core; they merit nothing better than such status descriptors."

If the Americans present an enigma to her, they too view her as "Jell-O, ice cream" lady from India, for she would not have any other food. The Americans eat chicken with its skin, whereas Indians would prefer it skinless. Her flawed English is noticed by the nurse Patty when she says 'finger and toe' for 'fingers and toes' because in Bengali language, the plural form is not different from the singular.

When it comes to naming the new-born, the Gangulis want Ashima's grandmother to "do the honours." In India, the elders in the family are respected and seeking their guidance in such a matter is considered to be obligatory on the young people. But, "In India, parents take their time. It wasn't unusual for years to pass before the right name, the best possible name, was determined. Ashima and Ashoke can both cite examples of cousins who were not officially named until they were registered, at six or seven, in school" (25).

Mr. Wilcox, the compiler of the hospital birth certificates, is at his wits' end in understanding the reason for the Gangulis not naming their child themselves. He wants to know the 'backup' name in case they do not like the name suggested by the grand-mother. But "Ashima and Ashoke shake their heads. It has never occurred to either of them to question Ashima's grandmother's selection to disregard an elder's wishes in such a way" (28).

There are some nasty experiences also in store for the immi-grants. Prejudices exist among natives towards the emigrants and vice versa. Commenting on the American bias against the South Asian writers on the whole, Siddharth Shanghvi says, "Her work is often classified neatly as immigrant fiction, and she is feted for writing about upwardly mobile South Asians, almost as if such an entity were a quaint oddity unto itself.[. . .] Perhaps such criti-cism inadvertently betrays the discrimination intrinsic to the American psyche, which identifies writers by colour or sexuality or gender, reducing writers, like tea leaves, to produce a wholly unpalatable brew, something to be ordered over the counter from one of its countless generic cafes."

The racial bias in America finds mention in the novel. As a child, Gogol had drawn the picture of his mother in which he had put a dot on her forehead to represent the *bindi* worn by the In-dian women. He had also pictured his father with his glasses and his little sister Sonia. When Mrs. Merton, the American babysit-ter has a look at it, she comments, "Well, if that's not the spitting image" (61). There is also another incident which shows how neighbourhood ruffians, driven by prejudices of colour and race, wreak havoc on the migrants. In case of the Ganguli family, it starts with the removal of the letters 'ULI' from the name 'GANGULI' written on the mail box of the Ganguli house on Pemberton Road. The ruffians have not just left 'GANG' but also added 'REEN' to it to denote 'GANGREEN' (American for Gangrene), which is the name of a dreaded disease. Gogol feels sick when he has a look at it. Before long, he gets used to "cash-iers in stores smirking at his parents' accent and of salesmen who prefer to direct their conversation to Gogol, as though his parents were either incompetent or deaf" (67-68). His father has, however, learnt to put up with this prejudiced behaviour of the Americans. Such maverick actions make the immigrants feel insecure and displaced and their inability to do anything in this regard makes them feel alienated from the mainstream society.

Of course, the inter-cultural relations are not all dyed in negativity. The power that Indian parents, particularly that which mothers wield over their children is an object of awe and respect for the Americans. Moushumi, as a teenager, felt duty-bound to call up her mother whenever she visited her friends without having previously informed her.

Similarly, the Indians also note the positive aspects of American life. An episode is described in which Ashima's shopping bags are left behind in the train and are retrieved later when Ashoke phones up the Lost and Found Department of the company running the trains. They get back all the bags with the contents perfectly in place. This aspect of American life impresses Ashima no end and she talks about it to her friends over the next few days. "Only in America," the phrase which she relished repeating while referring to the return of her shopping bags on the subway train, also found another context—this time not so attractive one—but then things are not the same everywhere. If there is no lock on the door at New Hampshire, in New York, Ashoke's car gets broken into in just five minutes and their suitcase is stolen.

The Americans are not all formal. When Ashima returns from the hospital with her newborn baby, the landlord's family arrives and they celebrate their homecoming with champagne. They have also brought broccoli quiche and a basket of old baby clothes which their daughters had once worn. The Americans intentionally put in words to show themselves informal even if they cannot take it in the long run. So, before leaving, Judy advises Ashima to "holler" if she needs anything. (34) As Ashima goes about the market with her infant in the perambulator, she is accosted by many an American who smilingly congratulate her on being a mother and ask about the baby, its name, sex etc. (34) When the Montgomerys learn about the death of Ashima's father, they leave a vase of flowers at their door as a mark of condolence. (46) Over a period of time, inter-mixing of cultures is inevitable. Therefore:

> Their garage, like every other, contains shovels and pruning shears and a sled. They purchase a *barbecue for tandoori* [emphasis added] on the porch in summer [. . .] They learn to roast turkeys, albeit rubbed with garlic and cumin and cayenne, at Thanksgiving, to nail a wreath to their door in December, to wrap woolen scarves around snowmen, to color boiled eggs violet and pink at Easter and hide them around the house. For the sake of Gogol and Sonia they celebrate, with progressively increasing fanfare, the birth of Christ, an event the children look forward to far more than the worship of Durga and Saraswati. (64)

Ashoke learns to buy ready-made suits now, exchanges fountain pen for ball pen etc. "In the supermarket they let Gogol fill the cart with items that he and Sonia, but not they, consume: individually wrapped slices of cheese, mayonnaise, tuna fish, hot dogs. For Gogol's lunches they stand at the deli to buy cold cuts, and in the mornings Ashima makes sandwiches with bologna or roast beef. At his insistence, she concedes and makes him an American dinner once a week as a treat, Shake'n Bake Chicken or Hamburger Helper prepared with ground lamb" (65). Their food habits are changing and the Americanization process is led by the children. "For when Ashima and Ashoke close their eyes it never fails to unsettle them, that their children sound just like Americans, expertly conversing in a language that still at times confounds them, in accents they are accustomed not to trust." (65)

Relocation

For the Indian parents who beget children in America, the acculturation of their children according to their home culture becomes problematic. They would love to see their children steeped in old Indian values, but then the milieu has its impact and the children unconsciously interiorize American values. At their age, it is so easy for the young generation to be influenced by their peer group. Once the children pass out of school and start earning, they do not stay with their parents. This fact has to be accepted by the parents. But for Ashima, it is nothing less than double whammy as the following passage explains:

> Having been deprived of the company of her own parents upon moving to America, her children's independence, their need to keep their distance from her, is something she will never understand. Still, she has not argued with them. This, too, she is beginning to learn. She had complained to her friends at the library, and they had told her it was inevitable, that eventually parents had to stop assuming that their children would return faithfully for the holidays. (166)

The Bengali community tries to educate their children. Ashima teaches Gogol Tagore's poem, names of deities and festivals etc. The Indian children are taught to call the family friend as 'uncle' or 'aunty.' Being Bengalis, Gogol is groomed to call Maya Nandi as Maya Mashi. In the Bengali class arranged by the expatriate Bengali community, Gogol is taught to read and write the alphabet used by his ancestors.

Being the son of Indian parents, Gogol is not supposed to take to American values. It is a matter of satisfaction for his parents that "Gogol does not date anyone in high school. He suffers quiet crushes, which he admits to no one, on this girl or that girl with whom he is already friends. He does not attend dances or parties. [. . .] His parents do not find it strange that their son doesn't date, does not rent a tuxedo for his junior prom. They have never been on a date in their lives and therefore they see no reason to encourage Gogol, certainly not at his age" (93).

Second Generation Diaspora

The experience of most second-generation South Asians settled in America shows that similar cultural background helps life partners to adjust to each other. They have shared history and locale to talk about. At the same time, prior expectation of men mired in tradition come a cropper if the spouse happens to have been impressed by the mainstream host culture. The first generation's story was about adaptation and learning, acculturating, and also discovering new things about themselves. The second generation finds itself presented with two conflicting realities and cultures and sets of expectations—one of the host country through the socio-cultural surroundings and the other of the home country through their parents.

Of particular interest, from the point of view of comparative study of the two cultures—American and Indian—is the phase in Gogol/Akhil's life in which he gets involved with his second girlfriend Maxine or Max. As the intimacy between the two deepens, Gogol is drawn into Maxine's family also since she resides with her parents after her break-up with her previous boyfriend. He likes the fact that after the break-up with her boyfriend, Maxine returned to her parents. He finds it "endearingly old-fashioned" though he cannot think of doing it in his own case. When Maxine had invited him to her home, he had hesitatingly sought to know of her parents' views, but then Maxine had blurted out: "Why on earth would they mind?"

When Gogol meets her parents Gerald and Lydia for the first time, what strikes him is the openness with which they talk with him. Gerald does not mind telling his guest to set the table for dinner. When Lydia has served food, Gogol finds it frugal as compared to the food served by his mother to their Bengali guests. Americans do not pester their guests to have more of this thing or that as the Indians do. The conversation revolves around the city of New York, its buildings, the Ratliffs' house etc. They also discuss movies, art exhibits, restaurants etc. which hardly interested Gogol's parents. "Gogol is unaccustomed to this sort of talk at mealtimes, to the indulgent ritual of the lingering meal, and the pleasant aftermath of bottles and crumbs and empty glasses that clutter the table" (134).

He often stays overnight in Maxine's room, but he is surprised to note that Maxine's parents do not mind it even slightly. This provides him an opportunity to learn the true American ways. "He learns that one does not grate Parmesan cheese over pasta dishes containing seafood. He learns not to put wooden spoons in the dishwasher, as he had mistakenly done one evening when he was helping to clean up" (137). He also notes that Maxine respects her parents' tastes and their ways. At the dinner table, she argues with them about books and paintings as she would with her friends. "There is none of the exasperation he feels with his own parents. No sense of obligation. Unlike his parents, they pressure her to do nothing, and yet she lives faithfully, happily, at their side" (138). Obviously, Gogol compares the two patterns of parents-children relationships and prefers the American to the Indian pattern. It is through his eyes that the family ties in each culture have been judged.

Maxine is surprised to learn that Gogol's parents have only Bengali friends, "that they had had an arranged marriage, that his mother cooks food everyday, that she wears saris and a bindi." (138). To Maxine it is "depressing." Gogol is upset at this reaction and wishes they could be like the Americans in their relationship but he cannot help it. Gogol's relationship with the Ratliff family deepens and he becomes almost its member. He helps them in arranging parties at the weekends. Gogol is also charmed with the American way of partying. There are normally around a dozen guests—a carefully selected mix of painters, editors, academics, gallery owners etc. They sit around the candlelit table and eat the meal, course by course, discussing various subjects intelligently. These parties are different from the ones thrown by his parents which are cheerful but also unruly because the number of people is not below thirty. There are children also. So, they have to eat in batches, invariably to the prodding of the host. Thus, while Gerald and Lydia seemed to preside at these dinners, his own parents, he feels, behaved more like "caterers in their own home, solicitous and watchful" (140). However, Gogol feels at times that "his immersion in Maxines' family is a betrayal of his own" (141) which shows he is not totally apathetic to the feelings of his parents.

In June every year, both Gerald and Lydia go to their lake house in New Hampshire. Gerald's parents live there throughout the year. Their departure reminds Gogol of his own family's annual visits to Calcutta but there is an important difference in that whereas the visits to India were paid as part of duty, here the Ratliffs visited New Hampshire only for the sake of pleasure. They have an old and musty house here with primitive and mismatched furniture. The pipes in the bathroom are not covered. The floor does not run from wall to wall. There are unshaven logs supporting the roof. In short, it is just opposite of how they lived in New York. To Maxine, however, "It's sort of like being at camp" (152). All day long, Gogol and Maxine walk about the house barefoot. Gogol goes for runs around the lake with Gerald. Gerald spends most of his time in his vegetable garden. Slowly, he starts appreciating this idyllic place and its disconnect with the outside world but he is doubtful if his parents would like such a life.

What is more, Maxine's parents are least concerned about the private life of their daughter. They do not have questioning looks when Gogol and Maxine emerge from their daughter's bedroom in the morning. This, of course, would be unacceptable to Indians of the first generation settled in America. The reserved manner in which Maxine had been received at Gogol's home presents a contrast here. Jhumpa Lahiri describes matter-of-factly the American life. She neither does idolize nor decry the American lifestyle, as for instance, the sexual relations between Gogol and his girl-friends.

But Maxine fails to grasp the intensity of suffering through which Gogol passes after the death of his father. The American viewpoint is reflected in Maxine's query if Gogol would not like to "get away from all this," to which Gogol replies in the negative. Thereafter, she quips, "What do you expect of me?" She continued to live with him for sometime but gradually she lost patience as Gogol would be silent at the dinner table and rather indifferent in bed. He was now more concerned about his mother and sister with whom he would converse telephonically every evening. He would go over to see them every weekend. He did not take her along, nor was she invited to go to Calcutta with the rest of the family. In this, Gogol was being too private and Maxine was being treated as an outsider even though she desired to be part of the family. The shock following his father's death had bereft him of his love for Maxine. Instead of analyzing his behaviour towards Maxine, Gogol walked out on her one day for good. Later, she got engaged to another person.

If Maxine, despite her faux pas in her attempt to wean Gogol away from grief over his father's death, was keen on adopting

Indian culture, there is the counterpoint in the second generation Indian immigrant who fails in imbibing her ancestral culture and crosses over to the American side. Moushumi presents an interesting case study of acculturation. The girl who, as a youngster, had kept herself aloof from others of her age; who charmed American mothers by her sense of duty towards her mother whenever she went out of her home to play with other children; who as a college student had only imagined but never savoured the company of young class-mates and professors, would totally give up her moorings and overshoot the coveted Americanization. She would change in Paris into one with least compunctions about sleeping with men. There would be no regard of age or race of these men. "She was exactly the same person, looked and behaved the same way, and yet suddenly, in that new city, she was transformed into the kind of girl she had once envied, had believed she would never become" (215). Clearly, at the psychological plane, she desired to be like the other, though she did not find herself adequately prepared for it.

Her job in Paris was to help American businessmen learn French and this came in handy to be intimate with them. Finally, she fell in love with Graham, an investment banker from New York who was living in Paris. For his sake, she joined the New York University. Both of them lived in New York, without letting their families know. When her parents came to visit her, he would disappear into a hotel "removing all traces of himself from the apartment" (216). Later, she introduced him to her parents who did not raise any objection because most of the other Bengali girls of her age in their friends' circle had been married off. Before marriage, Graham flew into Calcutta to meet the large number of Moushumi's relatives. Back in New Jersey, however, he was heard complaining in a merry company about his stay in Calcutta. He found the Indian culture "repressing" and the society "somewhat provincial." "Imagine dealing with fifty in-laws without alcohol," he said (217). Moushumi realized that he had been fooling everybody. They argued and differences cropped up between them. In a moment of rage, she took off the engagement ring and threw it into the street. Subsequently, Graham moved out of her apartment and her life. It put an end to Graham's attempt to assimilate. Indian culture and be integrated with the Indian community. This is another of the several situations created by Lahiri in the novel, like case-studies of different degrees of integration/ assimilation of immigrants in the host culture and vice versa. The present relationship reminds one of Kipling's famous line: "East is East and West is West / And never the twain shall meet.

An important aspect of diasporic life is the relationship between second generation youths exemplified by Gogol and Moushumi. Both were born of Indian parents and brought up outside India. Both of them had drunk deep of the liberal spirit flowing so freely in America but Moushumi was way ahead of Gogol. She was married to Gogol for which the parents of both the parties prepared ground. It was almost an arranged marriage and it went on well for sometime. There was no provocation from Gogol's side but Moushumi simply got bored of one man in her life. Fate brought an old acquaintance Dimitri to her and she started seeing him secretly. Now, extra-marital affair is something which is winked at neither in American culture nor in Indian. It could not have remained unnoticed by Gogol particularly because the frequency of Moushumi-Dimitri meetings had increased. One false move and the cat was out of the bag. Moushumi did not take long to get divorce from Gogol and be a free bird again. Coming from the same cultural background, Gogol and Moushumi were supposed to make the marriage a roaring success. In presenting this test-case, so to say, Lahiri seems to suggest the lack of commitment for the traditional values among the second generation immigrant youth.

Exile and Loneliness

The feeling of exile becomes acute for the immigrants when they find it practically impossible sometimes to be the co-sharers in joys and grief of relatives staying in home country. The young generation that has moved out of India to countries like America, has the old parents back in India. Due to strong family ties, both sides feel the absence of each other. When a close relative or one of the parents of the expatriate passes away and he or she is not able to fly back to India to be with the other members of the bereaved family, a feeling of remorse overtakes the immigrant. When Gogol leaves Cleveland for Boston with the ashes of his father, his state of mind is similarly described by Jhumpa Lahiri: "He knows now the guilt that his parents carried inside, at being able to do nothing when their parents had died in India, of arriving weeks, sometimes months later, when there was nothing left to do" (179).

Loneliness is a powerful theme in this novel and Lahiri has portrayed it in all its poignancy without over-sentimentalizing it. Away from home and kith and kin, each member of the Ganguli household leads a solitary life. Ashoke is busy from morning till evening at the university. Ashima has to find ways to keep herself engaged in order to avoid sense of void and solitude. Therefore, she spends time in the library of her son's school, taking employment there later. When Ashoke moves out to Cleveland, she has more time at hand and makes her own Christmas cards. A grown-up Gogol moves away from family but he too faces loneliness and is not able to retain any female partner for long. At the end of the novel, we find Gogol alone and his mother ready to don the mantle of a lone traveller.

For the diasporic, the exile becomes a permanent condition of homelessness. A single incident, a train accident becomes the leitmotif of the novel. Ashoke Ganguli, Gogol's father, had been urged by his grandfather, a professor of European literature, to read the Russians with the assurance that "They will never fail you." When the train he was riding outside Calcutta derailed, Ashoke was immersed in Gogol's stories. To Ashoke, it was Gogol the writer, who saved his life. Quoting Dostoyevsky's comment "We all came out of Gogol's overcoat," Ashoke had told his son, "It will make sense to you one day" (78). He will, therefore, feel redeemed if he leaves the India he loves. This was the message one could derive from Nikolai Gogol's life much of which was spent in exile and this is what Mr. Ghosh, the co-traveller in the ill-fated train carrying Ashoke told him as if reminding him of his grandfather's intimate desire. This is also taken to be Ashoke's way of paying tribute to his grandfather.

By showing Ashoke's death in America, Jhumpa Lahiri underscores the diasporic elements of spatial, emotional and cultural displacement as signifying a permanent condition of man. Ashoke's death provides Lahiri with the occasion to muse over the plight of the expatriates: "Who had forsaken everything to come to this country, to make a better life, only to die here?" (180). Ashima at first does not wish to go to Calcutta but wants to stay here where her husband breathed his last. This again indicates the value of sentiments and family ties in the life of Indians as against the practical Americans. But finally, she is overtaken by Ashoke's philosophy of life, which was also Nikolai Gogol's and Mr. Ghosh's and every immigrant's. She would, therefore, spend half a year in America and the other half in India. Gogol's future is still not chalked out; he carries on with another journey in his unsettled life. It answers perfectly to the Freudian perception of the melancholy of the diasporic, which is that "diaspora is like being ejected out of a mother's womb; you can't return to the womb, so you are condemned to a perpetual moving without arrival" (Vijay Mishra, qtd. Paranjape 60).

The Betrayal Motif

Siddharth Dhanvant Shanghvi, himself a novelist, finds *The Namesake* to be a tale of betrayal. It is this trait that overshadows the novel and not the diasporic element. In a review article captioned "The Betrayal Artist," he comments, "In her novel, *The Namesake*, parents are betrayed by children, who embraced new life—and a new nation—with an eagerness that is almost embarrassing. Embracing Americana is not inherently a disloyalty, but is experienced as that in its latent rejection of India, or more specifically, the mores of Bengali life, of Calcutta, of a past that will never return. The same children, when they return to their roots—going as far as to co-opt into an arranged marriage—are betrayed by this unfairly venerated institution, by their philandering Bengali spouse, and perhaps also by the parents who encouraged them to marry into the community."

Surprisingly enough, the writer Jhumpa Lahiri herself struggled with the motif of betrayal with regard to her identity. This is what she told an interviewer: "I really felt it would be a betrayal of my parents to call myself American." (Wiltz) This despite the fact that she was born in England and grew up in America but then it is not so simple a feeling. At its back lies the whole subconscious complex of experiences and certain inborn inclinations. Lahiri also recalls situations where people were not convinced if she told them she was American because of her Indian name and her brown colour.

Shanghvi rightly avers that the acceptance of American culture need not necessarily exclude Indianness. What he probably seems to support is the creolized form that comes out of the union of two cultures. In fact, seedlings of such a pattern sprout in the lifetime of the first generation itself when the Gangulis celebrate Christmas and observe Thanksgiving Day at home.

However, to find only the betrayal motif to the exclusion of other motifs in the novel, would be an exercise in reductionism. The so-called betrayal of his parents by Gogol was not final in any case. He did come under the impact of American culture through his peer group as he grew into a young man and imbibed a lifestyle that put premium on the physical rather than the emotional. But things had not worsened beyond repair. The emotional jolt provided by the unfortunate death of his father rejoined him to his mother and family. Coincidences do happen in life but this partial betrayal is off-set by complete betrayal of Gogol by his Bengali wife Moushumi. Do we believe that she had been completely Americanized? It would be naïve to dub betrayal as an American and fidelity as Indian value. Maxine, though failed to appreciate the Indian sensibility, yet she did not leave Gogol happily. And then how does one blame the institution of marriage for betraying the partners unless you wish to blame destiny. This institution requires a measure of marital discipline which those considering it "unfairly venerated" may not be able to appreciate.

Conclusion

Having said this, let us remind ourselves that the diasporic today is different from the diasporic of the past. He is not forcibly taken to the far off land from his moorings. In our times, the expatriate is the master of his own self. He migrates in search of better pastures to the technologically advanced society of the West. Under these circumstances the theories of yore hardly correspond to reality. Pointing to this insufficiency, a critic points out: "The constrictive categories (that have tended to be both proscriptive and prescriptive) that define and delineate the post-colonial and the diaspora also confine it to a space of liminality" (Bhattacharya 142).

Jhumpa Lahiri has presented relationships with varying degrees of acculturation of the second generation of Indian immigrants. The transformation cannot be viewed in terms of black and white, for they inhabit a liminal space of constant contestation and appropriation of culture of the adopted country of their parents. In any process of culturation, the possibility of change exists at all moments of life, so we get hybrid characters rather than pure subjectivities. Even when she speaks of the difference, her representation of difference "must not be hastily read as the reflection of pre-given ethnic or cultural traits set in the fixed tablet of tradition." This is so because, "The social articulation of difference, from the minority perspective, is a complex, on-going negotiation that seeks to authorize cultural hybridities that emerge in moments of historical transformation" (Bhabha 2). Even of the stability of these hybridities one cannot be sure, for the Hegelian dialectics does not admit of any homogenized stasis for long in history. Comments another critic: "The diaspora has to be conceptualized in similar terms, not as a historical exigency of 'hybridity' but a two-faced Janus that creates a distinct space for each culture it encounters" (Bhattacharya 149).

Similarly, with regard to the issue of identity, there is no doubt that it is not static and at any given moment, identity is under formation. We cannot really proclaim Moushumi a successful convert to a new culture and Gogol a denizen of the twilight region. In fact, we need to be cautious while labelling the diasporic as dislocated because, as Atanu Bhattacharya points out, "The expatriate's (the erstwhile exile or the diasporic intellectual) identity needs to resist the theorizing centripetal pull of 'dislocatedness'—a category that now defines, and therefore, delimits 'authentic marginality'—by counterpoising it with a 'relocatedness'—a ground that creates stability and equipoise, however fleeting that may be. The diaspora has now to be understood in terms of not as a site of contestation where ignorant (or not so ignorant) armies clash by night, but as a site of constellation—a space that provides equal weightage to the logic of exclusion (and exclusivity) as well as to the logic of identity" (142).

The novel is a comparative study of different cultures—of America and India mainly. From the very start, the focus is on comparing the lifestyle, milieu, landscape, facilities, thinking, rituals etc. of the two countries. Most of the cross-cultural relationships involving the key protagonists—Gogol-Ruth, Gogol-Bridget, Gogol-Maxine, Gogol-Moushumi, Moushumi-Graham have either not taken off to the marital terrain or have, after experimenting with live-in relationship, been rocked midway. Does the writer conform to Rudyard Kipling's averment: 'East is East and West is West and never the twain shall meet'? Actually, the writer does not quite draw the line here. The case of Sonia-Ben relationship has been left open, which shows there is room for experimentation and subsequent hope. This also gives the novel a postmodern context. In comparing this relationship with the Gogol-Maxine problematic relationship, the severity of the latter is sought to be diluted. In a globalized world, the multiculturalism relationship could be the norm rather than the exception, the author seems to suggest. It is the first generation immigrant community that insists upon maintaining links with their families left behind in India and undertaking cultural practices as also expecting their children to do likewise. If the second generation of Indian immigrants has been torn between two cultures, such a situation may not arise at all in case of the third generation, for as Gogol has shown, the second generation does not feel duty-bound to adhere to the cultural code of their parents' country. In problematizing the category of diasporic, Jhumpa Lahiri seems to be hinting at the irrelevance of the linkage of identity with race or nationality. "Ultimately, Lahiri anticipates the prevalence of a global identity that relies upon neither nationality nor ethnicity, but personal prerogative, an identity to be forged by the third generation and beyond" (Patil 149). At least, the cultural identity is open to reconstruction if not the political one which is a more rigid category.

Chapter 5

Characterization in *The Namesake*

Jhumpa Lahiri excels in the art of characterization with a balanced treatment of the external and inner details of her characters. An undercurrent of empathy runs through the narrative and this empathy is not limited to any particular type of individuals but is widely bestowed on all—young, old, Indians, Americans alike. Besides being subtly drawn, her characters belong to our times and our world. They are not wooden dummies or caricatures; they pulsate with life. There are enough details to render them individualized. Hence, they are substantial and not shadowy. Such characters endear themselves to the readers and leave a lasting impression on their minds. Lahiri's eye for detail coupled with a compassionate heart provides magic touch to the novel.

At the same time, we must not forget that her characters grow in a complex milieu, as they are located in the twilight region of differences woven by two cultures. According to Homi Bhabha, "It is in the emergence of the interstices—the overlap and displacement of domains of difference—that the intersubjective and collective experiences of *nationness*, community interest, or cultural value are negotiated" (2). Thus, the selfhood at the individual and collective level is never final; it is open to negotiation, collaboration and contestation. At any given moment, this identity is being defined/ re-defined.

Ashoke Ganguli

Ashoke is the father of the protagonist of the novel. Since, his youth, he has been a hard working person. The reader comes across Ashoke in the opening scene of the novel when he visits Ashima's house to have a glimpse of the girl whom he is to marry. He is described as "slightly plump, scholarly-looking but still youthful, with black thick-framed glasses and a sharp prominent nose" (8). He also sports a neatly trimmed moustache connected to a beard covering only chin. Wearing brown socks and brown trousers with a green-and-white-striped shirt, he has an aristocratic air about him.

It had been two years since he moved to the United States for studies. On this occasion, he had come back to India to get married. In Ashima's house, Ashoke does not speak a word. Instead, his father does all the talking. He tells about his son that he had graduated first-class-first from B.E. College. Presently, he lives in Boston, U.S.A. He has been studying there for his Ph.D. in fibre optics.

Ashoke was involved in a near-fatal train accident in October 1961, when he was traveling from Calcutta to Jamshedpur. Anyone else in his condition would have written his future off, because for one full year, he lay flat on his back—first three months in different hospitals and then at home. The next year, he returned to his college and graduated. He then applied for engineering studies abroad without taking anybody in the family in confidence. Despite protests from his parents and siblings, he reached U.S.A., which marks him as a person of strong will.

> Only after he'd been accepted with a full fellowship, a newly issued passport in hand, did he inform them of his plans. "But we already nearly lost you once," his bewildered father had protested. His siblings had pleaded and wept. His mother, speechless, had refused food for three days. In spite of all that, he'd gone. (20)

And yet it would be inhuman of him not to carry in his psyche the trace of terror of the bygone event. At times, certain outside stimuli make him re-live that nasty experience: "Seven years later, there are still certain images that wipe him flat. They lurk around a corner as he rushes through the engineering department at MIT, checks his campus mail. They hover by his shoulder as he leans over a plate of rice at dinner-time or nestles against Ashima's limbs at night" (20-21).

But the train accident also was responsible for the direction it gave to Ashoke's life. He had a chance meeting with one Mr. Ghosh, a co-traveller, who asked him if he had seen "much of the world." When Ashoke named Delhi and Jamshedpur, Ghosh advised him to think of seeing England, America etc. while he was still young and free. "Do yourself a favor. Before it's too late, without thinking too much about it first, pack a pillow and a blanket and see as much of the world as you can. You will not regret it. One day it will be too late," he told Ashoke (16).

Later, when he was rescued from the wreckage of the train, he felt he must redesign his life. Badly injured and lying amid the rubble that night, he heard the voices of the rescue party and was able somehow to raise his hand clutching a single page of the book he was reading, which act finally got noticed by the receding rescuers and he was pulled out. He felt the book *The Short Stories of Nikolai Gogol* was nothing less than a lucky talisman for him.

Nikolai Gogol had been Ashoke's source of inspiration. He had spent most of his life outside his country. While talking to his son, Ashoke adds proudly, "like me." He had read the story titled 'The Overcoat' included in that collection a number of times. It was the story of one Akaky Akakyevich, the impoverished man who spent his life copying documents written by others and suffering their ridicule. Ashoke found the image of his father in the protagonist, for he too, had been a petty clerk. Each time he read about the naming ceremony of Akaky and the rejection of several queer names by his mother, Ashoke laughed loudly, little knowing that he too would be held responsible for naming his son in a manner that would be considered queer by his son.

Gogol's christening was done at the spur of a moment when the hospital authorities cited rules to tell him that the new-born baby had to be given a name before Ashima and the baby could be discharged from the hospital. They had till then been waiting for a letter suggesting the name sent from Calcutta by Ashima's grandmother.

Ashoke is a loving father. He goes on outings with his children. There is specific mention of a visit to a lighthouse when he missed his camera and, therefore, asked Gogol to just remember the day and place, "where there was nowhere left to go" (187). They make a point of driving into Cambridge with the children when the Apu Trilogy plays are being staged at the Orson Welles, or when there is a Kathakali dance performance or a sitar recital at memorial Hall (65). Thus, he sees to it that they get to know about and like Bengali culture. He takes children along to Calcutta on several occasions. In an extended vacation of eight months in India, the children get to know India better.

After finishing his doctoral course, Ashoke takes up job as assistant professor of electrical engineering at a university. He moves his family into a house at 67, Pemberton Road which is to be their residence for the next twenty-seven years, the longest period of their life. In fact, it is while occupying this house that Ashoke passes away even though the death takes place in a university guest house where he had been staying ever since he took up a six-month research assignment.

Ashoke changes his lifestyle to keep up with the Joneses. "Accustomed to wearing tailor-made pants and shirts all his life, [he] learns to buy ready-made. He trades in fountain pens for ballpoints, Wilkinson blade sand his boar-bristled shaving brush for Bic razors bought six to a pack. Though he is now a tenured full professor, he stops wearing jackets and ties to the university" (65).

Ashoke comes out as a gentle and scholarly figure. His professional career shows a steady growth. It is on account of his scholastic aptitude and hard work that after completing his research work, he gets the job as a lecturer in the American university. He is a man of few words but he is firm in his resolve. When once he decides to leave India and study abroad, he can foresee his parents' opposition but he does not tell them. He has a dream which he is out to fulfill at any cost. This may not be taken as neglect of his parents because he never forgets to pay periodic visits to Calcutta to keep in touch with the members of his big family. He is a loving and caring husband and father. It is his tremendous love for his children that pulls Gogol back into his family.

What the reader is not able to know about Ashoke is his relationship with people beyond his close-knit family in America. Even of his extended family, one does not know much and about his colleagues at the workplace not a word is mentioned. There are references to the get-togethers of some Bengali families living in America on special occasions like birthdays of children or festival days which describe the hullabaloo and excitement associated with such affairs. They discuss, on these occasions, various topics like the American politics though they have no active role to play in it.

His is the life story of a true diasporic "who had forsaken everything to come to this country, to make a better life, only to die here" (180). However, the reader is not able to fathom Ashoke's mind. It would have been better if his viewpoint could have been made available to the reader through a peep into his stream of consciousness or indirect interior monologue. But perhaps Lahiri, being herself a young second generation member of the diaspora, found it more enticing and convenient to present the point of view of the youth.

Ashima Ganguli

Ashima presents the picture of a sober, subdued and traditional housewife. Her life presents very few instances of the ebullient or the exotic in married life. So far as her children are concerned, she performs her duties silently and scrupulously, without expecting anything in return.

The writer describes Ashima for the first time as a pretty and tall girl. Her complexion is on the "dark side of fair" (9). She resembles the film actress Madhabi Mukherjee. At the age of nineteen, she faces the prospect of being married to Ashoke, an Indian Bengali studying in the United States. As is common in India, the girl is given a brief test. In the present case, she is asked to recite a few stanzas from Wordsworth's poem 'The Daffodils' which she does dutifully. When asked if she was capable of living alone in that cold country, she poses the innocent counter-question: "Won't he be there?" (9).

The marriage ceremony does not take long to be solemnized and when she leaves in the company of her husband for America, there are a large number of her relatives at the airport to see her off. She reaches eight thousand miles away from her home to Cambridge, where she settles down to a routine in which her role is traditional—to wait for her husband to return from the university and to cook food for him. But the most gruelling experience is "motherhood in a foreign land" because it is to happen "so far from home, unmonitored and unobserved by those she loved" (6).

After the birth of her son, she wishes to go back to Calcutta to raise him there amongst her relatives but she knows she cannot do it for the sake of her husband. Alone at home, she tends her baby, singing lullabies to him and crying herself also, moved as she is by her lonely state. This sense of loneliness increases, when they move from the university apartments to a university town outside Boston. To her the entire stay in a foreign land appears nothing less than a life-long pregnancy, "a perpetual wait, a constant burden, a continuous feeling out of sorts" (49).

After her baby grows into a toddler, she takes him on Fridays to the public library for the children's story hour. To keep herself somewhat busy, once a week, she makes thirty samosas to be sold at the international coffeehouse, for twenty-five cents each. After Gogol turns four, she drops him off and fetches him from the university-run nursery school three mornings a week. When Gogol is at school, she passes time sullenly all by herself. She starts sitting in the reading room of the public library writing letters to her mother or reading magazines.

Two years after this, they move into their own house at 67, Pemberton Road. The neighbourhood is all American. Her Indian sense of cleanliness and purity is offended by their messy ways, like wearing shoes inside home but she can do little to change it. There are some Bengalis living in America with whom the Gangulis are in touch and on occasions like birthdays or festivals, they arrange get-togethers. Events like these do give them strength to live in this alien land. She also takes up the job of an assistant in a library to pass time since Gogol has grown up and joined school.

The problems of parenting do come her way. Gogol's name is a big problem for her son and therefore for her also. Much against their wishes, they cannot change the name at the school level. Finally, Gogol himself does it when he graduates. She also has a daughter named Sonia now but her growth does not cause any such problem. As a mother, Ashima performs her role very well. In this, she lives up to the image of an Indian mother. It is only when she expects her children to grow as traditional Bengalis that disenchantment lies in store for her. But then she learns her lesson which is that it is futile to expect children brought up in American milieu not to imbibe the spirit of America.

After the death of her husband, she does not wish to leave America because her husband breathed his last here. "Now I know why he went to Cleveland," she tells people, refusing, even in death, to utter her husband's name. "He was teaching me how to live alone." (183) She does what Ashoke had done. She would act true to her name which in Bengali means 'without boundary' and spend six months in India and six months in the United States.

By the end of the novel, Ashima has learnt to adjust with the reality of multiculturalism in America. Therefore, she approved of Ben as Sonia's husband. When Gogol had brought Maxine home, she was sceptical. She had not been able to put up with a prospective daughter-in-law who called her Ashima and her husband Ashoke. On the whole, she presents the image of an ideal, all-giving and all-suffering Indian mother. It is only towards the end that she plans to spend half-a-year in India and pursue her interest in music, but here also she does not assert her individuality, rather she follows in the footsteps of her late husband who idolized the life of a wanderer.

Gogol Ganguli

Gogol Ganguli is the central character in this novel. He is the namesake of Nikolai Gogol, the Russian writer and is the central consciousness around whom the diasporic tale of immigration of a Bengali couple is fabricated. He is the son of Indian American parents—Ashoke and Ashima. As a young man, he tries to adopt the mainstream culture of America but then rejecting one's own culture inherited from family is not so easy even in alien surroundings. He faces what Sharri Hallgren says "the dissonance of swerving between hip, fey American pop culture and the oppressive warmth of the extended Bengali community."

Gogol's identity was problematized first by his parents. In fact, Ashima had written to her grandmother to suggest a name for the newborn. In this way, she and her husband were honouring the Indian tradition where the head of the family is normally consulted in such matters. The grandma wrote back a letter but unfortunately, the letter got lost in transit. The hospital authorities, however, would not allow them to leave hospital without naming the newborn, in keeping with the rules. It was in these circumstances that Ashoke thought of the name of his beloved Russian author and named the baby 'Gogol' after him, believing that he was only giving his child a pet name. It is common in India for children to have one name given to them in infancy—a *daknam,* that stays on for domestic use, so to say, and another name—a *bhalonam*, that is given at the time of entry of the child into a school. This is the one by which the world knows him.

When Gogol was taken for admission to the kindergarten school, his parents wanted to give him a new name 'Nikhil.' However, Gogol could not answer questions put to him as Nikhil by the school Principal. Obviously, the new name had not been tried earlier. Once the parents were gone, the Principal ascertained the child's wish and finding him responsive to the name 'Gogol' entered it in the school record. The child seemed to like it but as he grew, he became aware of its uncommon characteristic.

Gogol slowly comes into his own. Howsoever hard the expatriate community may try to keep their children away from the culture of their adopted country, it is well nigh impossible for the youth not to be steeped in the milieu surrounding them. The first indication of Gogol's independent identity is reflected in his preference for displaying the gravestone drawings alongside his old ones in the kitchen. His mother refuses to display the rubbings in the kitchen alongside his other creations, his charcoal drawings and his magazine collages etc. She had never rejected her son's artwork even before, but "How can she be expected to cook dinner for her family with the names of dead people on the walls?" (71) But Gogol does not throw them away, instead he hides them in his room, for "these ancient Puritan spirits, these very first immigrants to America, these bearers of unthinkable, obsolete names, have spoken to him" (71).

His own name becomes a millstone round his neck which he cannot wish away. When Gogol is fourteen-year old, he is presented *The Short Stories of Nikolai Gogol* by his father, even though he would have preferred some other book. By now he has "come to hate questions pertaining to his name, hates having constantly to explain. He hates having to tell people that it doesn't mean anything 'in Indian'" (76). He even hates to wear the name on his sweater at school function because to him, it is absurd and obscure and has nothing to do with anything Indian or American. "At times his name, an entity shapeless and weightless, manages nevertheless to distress him physically, like the scratchy tag of a shirt he has been forced permanently to wear" (76).

On his birthday, however, his father enters his room with a gift, which is *The Short Stories of Nikolai Gogol.* Ashoke tells him about the importance of the novelist, saying that he spent most of his adult life outside his homeland like him but when he is about to refer to the train accident, he stops because, "his son's birthday, is a day to honour life, not brushes with death" (78). After Ashoke has gone, Gogol has a different perception of his name: "Not only does Gogol Ganguli have a pet name turned good name, but a last name turned first name. And so it occurs to him that no one he knows in the world, in Russia or India or America or anywhere shares his name. Not even the source of his namesake" (78). But this feeling does not stay for long.

Being the progeny of Indian parents, Gogol is not supposed to imbibe American values. It is a matter of satisfaction for his parents that "Gogol does not date anyone in high school. He suffers quiet crushes, which he admits to no one, on this girl or that girl with whom he is already friends. He does not attend dances or parties. [. . .] His parents do not find it strange that their son doesn't date, does not rent a tuxedo for his junior prom. They have never been on a date in their lives and therefore they see no reason to encourage Gogol, certainly not at his age" (93). But even as his parents smugly believe in his innocence, the fact is he has interiorized the influence of environment and has grown up like an American teenager. He smokes pot secretly with his companions and has started looking for girls. There is no logic given; it is just the influence of the peer group.

Gogol is serious about changing his name to Nikhil and for this purpose, he initiates legal proceedings. After all, tens of thousands of Americans changed their names every year. The change of name is granted and Gogol becomes Nikhil. He lets his friends and acquaintances know the new name. His parents also try steadily to change their way of addressing their son from Gogol to Nikhil, which, of course, gives birth to strange feelings in him. "But now that he's Nikhil it's easier to ignore his parents, to tune out their concerns and pleas." (105) Thus, he relates the nominal identity to behaviour.

Since he has adopted the new name himself, he feels he is the master of his own self and he need not be concerned about his parents' expectations of him. It may also be interpreted in another way also. We might see it as a sign of the coming of age in his case; he wishes to come out of the shadow of his parents and yearns for his independent identity. The peccadilloes or the more serious vices he indulges in may be seen in this light. "It is as Nikhil, that first semester, that he grows a goatee, starts smoking Camel Lights at parties and while writing papers and before exams, discovers Brian Eno and Elvis Costello and Charlie Parker. It is as Nikhil that he takes Metro-North into Manhattan one weekend with Jonathan and gets himself a fake ID that allows him to be served liquor in New Haven bars. It is as Nikhil that he loses his virginity at party at Ezra Stiles" (105). The act mentioned last also bears the stamp of an understatement thereby highlighting the seriousness attached to it in both the cultures. Sharri Hallgren comments about this phase of his life: "As Gogol moves into young adulthood, he becomes that classic: the charmingly spazzy, high-achieving mild depressive who doesn't yet comprehend how alluring he is to women. It is women—of varying caliber, but pistols one and all—who take him by the lapels, shake him awake to life's charms and inject the chronology of his life with some zest."

The climax is reached when Maxine visits Gogol's small and economically done flat located in a noisy area and finds it "awful." She asks him to stay with her. The prospect of staying with her thrills him no end. Gogol inhabits the transcultural space; his Americanization process is in fast forward mode. He had, in fact, always been ashamed of his Indian part of identity. How he undervalued it was evident when he failed to find, as a school kid, any Indian buried in the graveyard. In the college too, he had refrained from joining the association of Indian students.

Gogol's next relationship develops with Moushumi Mazoomdar whom he meets on his mother's insistence. They meet at a bar and have drinks and even though Gogol had not been serious about this meeting, their shared memories of past provide them with enough material to talk about. This familiarity arouses Gogol's interest in her. He takes her to a French restaurant and entertains her to dinner. Before bidding farewell, Gogol asks her if they should make their parents happy by meeting again to which Moushumi consents after a moment's thought. He continues to think of her in the following days and feels happy recalling her visits as a teenager to his home: "He struggles but fails to recall her presence at Pemberton Road; still, he is secretly pleased that she has seen those rooms, tasted his mother's cooking, washed her hands in the bathroom, however long ago" (200). Next time, when Moushumi offers him her scarf because Gogol is feeling quite cold and the former refuses out of modesty but later regrets, we find him feeling the first experience of romantic love.

Gogol is a Casanova of sorts. Ruth, Maxine, Bridget—there does not seem to be any end to the girls he beds easily. Moushumi is the latest but he not only walks with her to the bed room but to the altar as well. The marriage ceremony is performed according to traditional Bengali custom. As such, the parents of both the parties are extremely happy.

Slowly, Gogol gets disillusioned about Moushumi. Her excessive smoking habit is just one issue. These days, the stale smell of it [smoke], in her hair and on her fingertips, and in the bedroom where she sits typing, slightly disgusts him. Gogol also does not like it when she reveals that she stayed with Donald and Astrid for two months after her break-up with Graham. The question comes to his mind if he was making Moushumi happy. As it is, they do not argue, still have sex and she does not accuse him but "more and more he sensed distance, her dissatisfaction, her distraction" (272).

At a party where they are discussing naming of newborn children, Moushumi blurts out the secret that Nikhil had changed his name. He is stunned, for he had not expected her to tell about it to anyone since it reminded him of the near fatal accident involving his father and of his own guilt in changing his name now that his father is dead.

In 1999, Gogol and Moushumi had a divorce. The reason is her infidelity. She had started meeting an old acquaintance Dimitri secretly thrice a week and meeting for her meant having physical relations too. But while going along with Gogol to spend Christmas with his mother, Moushumi is caught on the wrong foot and her secret is out. As a result, the marriage is on the rocks. Even after a year of this episode, Gogol retains a sense of failure and shame. But then he realizes that he cannot blame her for making a cuckold of him, for he too, has acted on the same impulse.

Gogol now takes up a job with an architecture firm in New York. His job is to work with a team on designs for hotels, museums, corporate houses etc. He works late into evenings and gets paid quite handsomely. It is in New York that he gets involved with his second girlfriend Maxine or Max. As the intimacy between the two deepens, Gogol is drawn into Maxine's family also as she resides with her parents after her break-up with her previous boyfriend. Her house, which is aesthetically designed, is also full of numerous artifacts and well-crafted pieces of furniture. As an architect Gogol feels interested in all these things. He visits her formally when he is invited by her. He not only falls in love with Maxine but also with her parents and the house. "He loves the mess that surrounds Maxine, her hundreds of things always covering her floor and her bedside table, her habit" (137). He is also impressed by the open exhibition of love by Maxine's parents. He stays with her at night on a number of occasions and is physically involved with her. But her parents do not seem to mind it.

But his father's death puts a stop to this process. When the news reaches him through Sonia's phone call, he is at Maxine's and has just returned from dinner out. He takes a plane and reaches Cleveland to claim his father's body. At the hospital, he is his normal self, noting the lack of any magazines in the waiting room and feeling hungry at the sight of the food cart in the elevator. After having identified the body in the morgue, he reaches the apartment where his father had been staying. It is here that the seriousness of the loss overwhelms him. Thinking of his father living here alone these past three months, he feels the "first threat of tears." (174)

Gogol had developed the habit of obeying Maxine out of habit by now. Surprisingly, much against her urgings and his explicit promise to her, he decides to spend the night at his late father's apartment. Lying on the couch, his mind tries to guess the sequence of events leading to his father's death. Next day, when he takes the flight to reach Boston where his mother, sister and some friends of the family would be waiting for him, he feels terrified. He feels guilty, for he could do nothing for his father but then "He knows now the guilt that his parents carried inside, at being able to do nothing when their parents had died in India, of arriving weeks, sometimes months later, when there was nothing left to do" (179). This thought comforts his ruffled soul but the first experience of remorse at his lack of regard for parents indicates his coming of age.

Gogol stays with his mother and sister for the ten-day long mourning period. On the eleventh day, Maxine calls and is told by him that he would not be coming to New Hampshire. Clearly, the sad event has meant a turning point in his life. Everything connected to his father now comes to his mind at the slightest pretext. While journeying back to New York after his father's death, the slight tilt of the rails reminds him of the train accident which nearly killed his father: "In that brief period of suggested peril, he thinks always of that other train he has never seen, the one that had nearly killed his father. Of the disaster that has given him his name" (184).

When Gogol comes back to New York after his father's death, he rents an apartment on Amsterdam Avenue. He continues working for his old firm. Maxine stays with him for sometime but gradually she loses patience as Gogol would be silent at the dinner table and rather indifferent in bed. He was now more concerned about his mother and sister with whom he would converse telephonically every evening. He would go over to see them every weekend. He does not take her along, nor is she invited to go to Calcutta with the rest of the family. In this, Gogol was being too private and Maxine was being treated as an outsider even though she desired to be part of the family. The shock following his father's death had bereft him of his love for Maxine. Instead of analyzing his behaviour towards Maxine, Gogol walks out on her one day for good.

Towards the end of the novel, Gogol is shown realizing that his parents lived in America "in spite of what was missing" and now that he seems to be facing the same prospect of missing his only parent alive, he feels he lacks the stamina for it. Even though he had stayed deliberately away from his parents, yet he hovered close enough to his house. Only when his father moved to Cleveland, was he a little more away from him. He realizes that he came home for the sake of his family only. That means he was unconsciously tied to his family even as he interiorized the ways of the peer group—the American youth. It is the repressed part of his consciousness that is showing itself now. Along with the physical part, the emotional part of his self seems to have been inherited from his Indian parents. It is no less than a revelation to him.

At the last function held on the Pemberton Road, where the Gangulis had spent 27 years, Ashima asks Gogol to bring the camera and get some photographs. He goes upstairs to get his father's Nikon camera. There are so many things lying there, out of which he picks up a book—*The Short Stories of Nikolai Gogol*—which had been presented on his birthday by his father. It still bears the inscription: "For Gogol Ganguli" and alongside are the words in his father's hand: "The man who gave you his name, from the man who gave you your name." Gogol realizes that after his mother is gone, the name Gogol Ganguli will vanish from the lips of his loved ones and so, "cease to exist" (289). This is disconcerting rather than reassuring for him. His loss is much more at the end: his wife has deserted him, his father is dead and his mother too leaves him to lead an independent existence. He is thus lonely, distressed and displaced—indeed in an unenviable position. But he does not want his mother to cancel her plan to hop between India and America. Somewhere, the legacy of the diasporic left behind by his father is sought to be reclaimed by him. He has come to possess the will to pursue his dream of making it big as an architect single-handedly and creating his own identity. This is the kind of dream that brings numberless migrants from far and wide to America and he happens to be the second generation of one such immigrant.

Gail Caldwell rightly comments, "Lahiri presents her protagonist throughout the novel as Gogol, only calling him Nikhil when he's perceived through the eyes of an assimilated lover. This understated shift in viewpoint is perfectly executed, and it speaks to Lahiri's empathic grasp of the bargains and sorrows that accompany the flight of any phoenix. Humbled by the twists and turns across two continents that have all but defined the Gangulis, Gogol thinks to himself toward the end of the novel that "his family's life feels like a string of accidents, unforeseen, unintended." But then this is the definition of any life lived outside the strictest margins of safety—all of us victims of circumstance and of the mere blink of time. In its generous, exacting portrait of the clash between cultural dictates and one man's heart, *The Namesake* manages to transcend the limits of both."

The novel can be viewed as a typical coming-of-age story, that draws on common rather than uncommon experiences in the American context. Gogol takes initiative in most vital case involving identity crisis; he goes in for the name change but somehow the burden of the old name is not off-loaded. Hence the mental pressure becomes all the more acute.

Moushumi Mazoomdar

One of the major characters in the novel, Moushumi comes out as a beautiful, sensuous and an intellectually accomplished girl, who oversteps the limits of freedom. Her lack of commitment and rootlessness are evident in her numerous affairs with men and ultimately in her breakdown of marriage with Gogol. Hers is an interesting psychological study, for she reacts strongly against any restriction on her impulses and instincts.

Moushumi is an academic by profession. She has always been interested in studies. As a teenager, she opted for Jane Austen's novel rather than the television at the birthday party at Gogol's house. Later, when Gogol's mother told him about her from the point of view of matrimonial alliance, she was doing her Ph.D. in French literature at the New York University. Later, she taught French and participated in seminars in Paris. On her first wedding anniversary, Moushumi had passed her oral exam which means she had met all other requirements and had to submit dissertation only (ABD = All But Dissertation). She was awarded a research scholarship to work on her dissertation in France for one year.

Moushumi is the daughter of the Mazoomdar couple who are friendly with the Gangulis. Both the families are Bengalis residing in America. They had lived for a while in Massachusetts and then moved to New Jersey. Gogol remembered calling her mother 'Rina Mashi' and her father Shubir Mesho. She is introduced in the novel as a school-going teenager. At a party in his house, she is asked to go and watch the television with other children and her response is: "I detest American television." Her

British accent becomes a matter of joke among the youngsters gathered there. They hardly talk long enough at that time.

The American mothers were greatly charmed by the sense of duty displayed by young Moushumi, who would call her mother whenever she went out of her home to play with other children. But as she grew up, she imbibed American values. Although her parents tried to cultivate her as a demure Bengali girl fit for a Bengali husband, she "had made a pact with two other Bengali girls she knew, never to marry a Bengali man" (213). As she entered adolescence, her parents tried to get her engaged and with this end in view invited Bengali bachelors to their home but Moushumi never liked this. She did not even bid them goodbye when they left her home.

But this resolve did not take long to melt. Even as she rebuffed the Indian men in whom she did not feel interested, she was attracted towards fellow students and even professors. In a way, natural instincts asserted and her conscious self could not stand up to the demands of Freudian Id. And yet at the end of her college education, she had no boy-friend. Now she regretted having been too prudish in the past: "She regrets herself as a teenager. She regrets her obedience, her long, unstyled hair, her piano lessons and lace-collared shirts. She regrets her mortifying lack of confidence, the extra ten pounds she carried on her frame during puberty" (214).

The writer explains the psychological development because of which she turned to the study of French. In opting for this course, she had gone against the wishes of her parents. This was her "refuge." Now, she allowed men to seduce her in cafes, parks or museums. She allowed them to buy her drinks, dinners etc. and to take her to their apartments later. This was done with a vengeance. It did not matter if the man seducing her was a married man and a father. There were Germans, Persians, Italians among them but most of all these were French. Even in the span of a day, she slept with one man after lunch, another after dinner. "They were a bit excessive" she told Gogol and in the permissive society of America, of which both were the products, Gogol did not mind it. So, if Gogol was a Casanova, she was no less. In this, both of them had been steeped deep in the dye of American culture.

Her affair with Graham started during this phase. It was a serious affair. Her job in Paris was to help American businessmen learn French and this came in handy to have her numerous affairs. Finally, she fell in love with Graham, an investment banker from New York who was living in Paris. For his sake, she joined the New York University. Both of them lived in New York, without letting their families know. When her parents came to visit her, he would disappear to a hotel "removing all traces of himself from the apartment" (216). Later, she introduced him to her parents who did not raise any objection because most of the other Bengali girls of her age in their friends' circle had been married off.

Before marriage, Graham flew into Calcutta to meet the large numbers of Moushumi's relatives. Back in New Jersey, however, he was heard complaining in a merry company about his stay in Calcutta. He found the Indian culture "repressing" and the society "somewhat provincial" (217). "Imagine dealing with fifty in-laws without alcohol," he said. Moushumi realized that he had been fooling every body. They argued and differences cropped up between them. In a moment of rage, she took off the engagement ring and threw it into the street. Subsequently, Graham moved out of her apartment and her life. After her break-up with Graham, she was devastated. She refused to move into her parents' house, instead she stayed for two months with Donald and Astrid at their Brooklyn home. But she did not tell Gogol about it. It was only much later at a party at Donalds that her break-up was revealed by Donald. Moushumi's psyche is further sought to be explored by the writer in these words:

> By the time she'd met him she'd begun to fear that she was retreating into her former self, before Paris—untouched, bookish, alone. She recalled the panic she'd felt, all her friends married. She'd even considered placing a personal ad. But he had accepted her, had obliterated her former disgrace. (249)

Gogol's mother tells him that Moushumi lives in New York. She was supposed to have been married a year ago but then she had a break-up with her American fiancé. This happened after the hotel for the ceremony had been booked and the invitations sent. In order to humour his mother, Gogol agrees to see her. Moushumi has a thin face, pleasing features and straight brows. She has made up her eyes the way old heroines used to. Moushumi has a parting in the middle of her hair and she has gathered her hair into a chignon (*choti*). She wears glasses made of tortoise shell. Smoking seems to be her weakness and at times she proves herself a wine-guzzler also.

She is a studious type and always carries a book along to read during free time. Even when Gogol reaches the bar to meet her, she is lost in a book. Though it is a blind date engineered by their mothers, they develop a liking for each other. They talk about so many things—Gogol's bereavement, the house in which his mother lives, Moushumi's life in New York etc. She can recollect minutely the details of the house which she had visited as a teenager. She has been living in New York for the past two years, supporting herself with mofussil jobs. She stayed in Paris also but came to New York for the sake of her lover who later ditched her. Gogol remembers that she ignored him at his graduation party at which she was a guest. Even though Gogol had not planned it, he invites her to dinner at a different restaurant.

Her marriage with Gogol was an arranged one for which initiative was taken by their parents. She retained her independent identity by not changing her surname to Ganguli after her marriage to Gogol. She was also not in favour of having a hyphenated surname 'Mazoomdar-Ganguli' whose length would be awesome to her. But when her relatives in India address letters to "Mrs. Moushumi Ganguli," she shakes her head and sighs. Life after marriage goes on smoothly for a while. They party a lot and enjoy life but then the familiarity that had brought them together, sets down working against this intimacy.

At a party at Brooklyn, she commits the imprudent act of revealing Gogol's real name with which he was born. He had not expected her to tell about it to anyone since it reminds him of the near fatal accident involving his father and of his own guilt in changing his name now that his father is dead. He had told her the history of this name and she had said she understood it well. But now she had breached this understanding in such an insensitive manner. It had become a joke to an inebriated Moushumi.

There is mutual trust and respect between Gogol and Moushumi. She values his judgement in matters concerning designs of homes and objects. While they are sauntering up the Fifth Avenue in New York, she asks for his opinion about certain shoes. When he values them less than what she had in mind, she starts walking away but then reverts to see Gogol riveted to the shoe-window. She is impressed with the way Gogol had given consideration to her view after all. She appears faithful to her husband having revealed her past to him. Moreover, on their first wedding anniversary, Moushumi has been awarded a research scholarship to work on her dissertation in France for one year but she decides not to avail of it. For a while the reader is assured of her seriousness in matters concerning marriage but, before long, she succumbs to the pressure of her instincts. She wants to reassure herself that she could still be independent. Her mental conflict arising due to her individualistic attitude and her desire to enjoy the fruit of married life is portrayed in these lines:

> And yet the familiarity that had once drawn her to him has begun to keep her at bay. Though she knows it's not his fault, she can't help but associate him, at times, with a sense of resignation, with the very life she had resisted, had struggled so mightily to leave behind. He was not who she saw herself ending up with, he had never been that person. Perhaps for those very reasons, in those early months, being with him, falling in love with him, doing precisely what had been expected of her for her entire life, had felt forbidden, wildly transgressive, a breach of her own instinctive will. (250)

Once Moushumi has experienced male company, there is no looking back for her. In this, no moral considerations come her way. She is a weak-willed creature and is controlled by basic instincts only. It shows even on the dining table. When Dimitri orders a salad topped with warm lambs' tongue, a poached egg, and pecorino cheese, she swears she would not touch any item but "ended up eating the better part of" (264).

So far it could be condoned but she is a habitual violator of discipline of any type. She does have pangs of conscience at times but these are transitory: "She wonders if she is the only woman in her family ever to have betrayed her husband, to have been unfaithful. This is what upsets her most to admit: that the affair causes her to feel strangely at peace, the complication of it calming her, structuring her day" (266).

Her break-up with Gogol takes place in 1999. It is a coincidence that following the death of the mail attendant, Moushumi was sorting the mail in her department when her eyes fell on a letter addressed to a faculty from Dimitri, an old acquaintance from her school days. She is curious about him and contacts him. As had been her wont, it does not take long for her to enter the bedroom with him. She starts meeting him twice and then thrice a week without arousing Gogol's suspicion. But while going along with Gogol to spend Christmas with his mother, Moushumi is caught on the wrong foot and her secret is out.

They were going to spend Christmas with his mother and Sonia. Moushumi favoured renting a house in Siena along with Donald and Astrid but Gogol was not in favour of it. At that moment, she had blurted out, "Dimitri says Siena is something out of a fairy tale" (282). What happened was really dramatic: "Immediately, a hand had gone to her mouth, accompanied by a small intake of breath. And then, silence. 'Who's Dimitri?' he'd asked. And then: 'Are you having an affair?' . . . But as soon as he asked it, he knew" (282). The answer was not given but was rightly taken as "Yes." He felt sick that night. He did not tell his mother but suffered silently. However, she told him the whole story and "for the first time, another man's name upset Gogol more than his own" (283). The day after Christmas, she left Pemberton Road on the pretext of some interview. When he reached back, he found her belongings missing from the apartment. She had left for ever. Later, she did meet him in his office to get the divorce papers signed.

Moushumi is, thus, a typical postmodern rootless girl. For her, there is no question of getting tied to a centre. Neither family nor culture can bind her. What is more, she shows a disconnect with her own self also. Therefore, she acts erratically, impulsively as in the restaurant scene towards the end of the novel.

Chapter 6

Style in *The Namesake*

"Lahiri's short story collection, *Interpreter of Maladies*, won the 2000 Pulitzer Prize, and her deeply knowing, avidly descriptive, and luxuriously paced first novel is equally triumphant," declares Donna Seaman. There is no doubt that as in her earlier work, the art of story telling revolves around description and narration rather than the dramatic element of dialogue. It reminds one of the Victorian style of character portrayal through scenes and situations, persons and places. Lahiri is a painstaking writer and it is reflected in her prose that tries to create a balance between the internal and the external aspects, between the landscape and the mindscape. The *Library Journal* critic finds the novel "A rich, stimulating fusion of authentic emotion, ironic observation, and revealing details."

Jhumpa Lahiri's maiden novel has received rave reviews ever since it was published in the year 2003. Whereas the theme of the novel has its contemporary relevance, of no less importance is the way in which the subject matter has been moulded. She has been a teacher of creative writing and a discerning reader can mark the carefully laid out narrative plan as also the strategic use of different elements to introduce realistic, emotional and decorative situations that novel writing demands. And yet such a thing would be easier said than done, for no artist can bank purely upon cerebration, disregarding inspiration. When it was suggested to her in an interview that the moments of revelation or realization emerged slowly but surely in some of her stories and she was asked how she worked up "an illuminating moment in a character's life," she responded: "I really can't explain how I write, or what I'm thinking of consciously. I studied literature for so long, and was taught all of these things so deeply, all too well. I was trained to read stories, and to appreciate these elements, but when I write the stories I become a different person altogether. Everything goes out the window, and nothing applies in that sense." (Owens) In the same interview, she compares writing with child-birth which is not possible to accomplish through mere reading of notes.

The Plot

The novel covers a long time span of thirty four years in the life of the Ganguli family. It starts in 1968 but goes back, through a flashback, by two years when Ashoke got married to Ashima and brought her to America. There is also a reference to a train accident involving Ashoke that took place in the wee hours of October 20, 1961. The last chapter of the novel is laid in the year 2000. *The Namesake* is divided in ten chapters which are marked numerically only and do not bear any descriptive sub-title. Lahiri's narrative moves lightly through time, landing on selected years, as one would move through the pages of a photo album. Her point of view shuttles between the parents and their son, and is richly sympathetic to both generations. In this regard, Gail Caldwell's remark seems quite apt: "Sometimes Lahiri is heavy-handed in evoking the chasms between two cultures, and she has a tendency to leap elliptically from one of Gogol's life changes—his girlfriends, his life in New York as a young man—to the next. But more often the narrative displays an intelligence and care that reveal the depths of her characters and the hurdles they face with intricate ease."

In tracing the family history of the Gangulis over two generations, Lahiri seems to derive inspiration from Anton Chekhov. Some of the important events including deaths and funerals of Ashoke as also of the relatives back in Calcutta are only reported. Similarly, when it comes to arguments between Gogol and Ashoke or between Gogol and Moushumi, economy of language becomes the guiding principle. While suggestiveness is always a virtue in literary treatment, this becomes a hurdle at times in the complete absorption of the reader in the experience of the characters.

The plot is tenuous. It hinges on the name 'Gogol' given by Ashoke Ganguli to his son after an old Russian author. Gogol has to endure a Russian name that is acceptable neither to Indians nor to Americans. This alone provides the novel its exquisite and subtle tension that spans two generations and two continents and a plethora of emotional compromises in between. This, by itself, does not appear to be such a significant issue to the reader until its symbolic status in the context of the immigrant experience is established. The reasons for naming the baby-boy as 'Gogol' are complicated. They involve the horrendous 1961 wreck of the Howrah-Ranchi express that almost killed Ashoke in his youth, his subsequent recovery, and his moving over to the United States to pursue education at the MIT. Ashoke often struggles to express his reasons. When at last he tells his son the story, it has a profound effect on the boy, who until then had hated his strange name, and this marks a change in their relationship. The novel portrays beautifully the conflict between individual inclination and family loyalty.

Ashoke's death fills the void due to paucity of plot to a great extent. The story-line sustains after this event and the novel takes on a sombre tone with Gogol showing more responsible nature even though there is no end to his misfortunes. An interesting Americanized female character Moushumi, who becomes Gogol's wife briefly, is introduced. In the end however, we find that the diasporic motif of everlasting journey is writ large.

The story could be viewed as a series of episodes that could stand on their own as short stories, but they serve to introduce and build up the characters of Ashoke and Ashima and of their son Gogol. After Gogol moves away from home, the narrative takes us with him on his lonely journey through a rather unfair terrain of bad luck and tragedy. Eventually, he begins to find answers to some of his deep-seated questions.

Narrative Style

Jhumpa Lahiri has chosen simple present (indefinite) tense for her narrative, which fits in well with the Eastern art of storytelling. It is her way of discarding all temporal differentiations. The tense changes in the first chapter to record the flashbacks of the train accident and Ashoke's visit to Ashima's place before marriage. It also changes briefly in the last chapter when Gogol is shown in the bedroom of his father, reading *The Short Stories of Nikolai Gogol*. The story is related in future tense for a while before the author returns to the present tense and immediately after that the story is discontinued.

Even though Lahiri has taken care to lay equal emphasis on the external landscape and the internal mindscape, her narrative style is reminiscent more of the old novelists. She herself likes Chekhov, James Joyce, Thomas Hardy, Nathaniel Hawthorne and Hemingway among others. Surprisingly, her style is not influenced by Nikolai Gogol, whose story 'The Overcoat' occupies a seminal place in the novel, as she herself remarked in an interview: "I don't turn to Gogol as consistently as I do to certain other writers when I'm struggling with character or language. His writing is more overtly comic, more antic and absurd than mine tends to be" (Das). Among the living writers, she admits to being impressed and inspired by James Joyce, William Trevor, Alice Munro, Mavis Gallant et al.

In depicting petty details of domestic chores, she simulates Jane Austen but she does not go in for Austen's stress on dialogue in the novel. In the closing chapter, Ashima Ganguli is preparing for a party prior to her leaving for India:

> Alone, she manages an assembly line of preparation. First she forces warm boiled potatoes through a ricer. Carefully, she shapes a bit of the potato around a spoonful of cooked ground lamb, as uniformly as the white of a hard-boiled egg encases its yolk. She dips each of the croquettes, about the size and shape of a billiard ball, into a bowl of beaten eggs, then coats them on a plate of bread crumbs, shaking off the excess in her cupped palms. Finally she stacks the croquettes on a large circular tray, a sheet of wax paper between each layer. She stops to count how many she's made so far. She estimates three for each adult, one or two for each of the children. Counting the lines on the backs of her fingers, she reviews, once more, the exact number of her guests. Another dozen to be made, she decides. She pours a fresh heap of bread crumbs on the plate, their colour and texture reminding her of sand on a

beach. She remembers making the first batches in her kitchen in Cambridge. (274)

Inscape Portrayal

The stream of consciousness technique has become an integral part of the contemporary novel. Jhumpa Lahiri also uses it to enlighten the reader about the goings-on in the mind of her character. We have a glimpse of Gogol's state of mind with the author using the cinematic device of 'zoom in' on the particular moment when he heads for New York by train for the first time after his bereavement. The scene from the train window spurs the chain of thought: "It is a view his father would have appreciated, and Gogol is reminded of the many times he had driven with his family, on cold Sunday afternoons to the sea There were times when it had been so cold that they had simply sat in the car, in the parking lot, looking at the water, his parents sharing tea from a thermos in the front seat, the engine running to keep them warm. Once they had gone to Cape Cod, driving along that curving piece of land until they could drive no farther. He and his father had walked" (185).

At places, Jhumpa Lahiri's use of the stream of consciousness technique reminds one of Virginia Woolf's use of it in *Mrs. Dalloway*, in which the protagonist of this eponymous novel sets out for the market in the morning: "Though the day is bright for a change, it is particularly cold, brisk air stinging his ears. He remembers his first lunch with Moushumi, the afternoon she'd dragged him to the hat store. He remembers the two of them crying out in unison as the wind blasted their faces, a time too soon for them to cling to each other for warmth. He walks now to the corner. [. . .] Suddenly, he wants to go back to the apartment, climb into the loft bed and forget about sightseeing, hold Moushumi in his arms. He wants to lie with her for hours, as they did at the beginning, skipping meals, then wandering the streets at odd hours, desperate for something to eat. But she must present her paper at the end of the week, and he knows she will not be roused from her task of reading it aloud, timing its duration, making small marks in the margin. He consults his map" (232).

Such mixing of reminiscence and reverie truly illuminates the recesses of the psyche of any character.

Memories cross Moushumi's mind also as she sorts out mail immediately after the death of the mail attendant Alice at the NYU. The job reminds her of how she relished organizing things as a child: "As a child she always had a knack for organization; she would take it upon herself to neaten closets and drawers, not only her own but her parents' as well. She had organized the cutlery drawer, the refrigerator. These self-appointed tasks would occupy her during quiet, hot days of her summer vacation, and her mother would look on in disbelief, sipping watermelon sherbet in front of the fan" (256). In fact, the indirect interior monologue has been used copiously as a strategy to make up for the dearth of direct dialogues in the novel. Siddharth Shanghvi subscribing to the similarity between Jhumpa Lahiri and Virginia Woolf, remarks: "Reading Lahiri is an illuminating experience of Woolf's almost visceral, and ultimately realized aspiration."

Ashima's relationships are traced through a peep into her mind in the following lines:

> She passes over two pages filled only with the addresses of her daughter, and then her son. She has given birth to vagabonds. She is the keeper of all these names and numbers now, numbers she once knew by heart, numbers and addresses her children no longer remember. She thinks of all the dark, hot apartments Gogol has inhabited over the years, beginning with his first dorm room in New Haven, and now the apartment in Manhattan with the peeling radiator and cracks in the walls. Sonia has done the same as her brother, a new room every year ever since she was eighteen, new roommates Ashima must keep track of when she calls. She thinks of her husband's apartment in Cleveland, which she had helped him settle into one weekend when she visited. She'd brought him in expensive pots and plates, the kind she used back in Cambridge, as opposed to the gleaming ones from Wiliams-Sonoma her children buy for her these days as gifts. Sheets and towels, some sheer curtains for the windows, a big sack of rice. In her own life Ashima has lived in only five houses: her parents' flat in Calcutta, her in-laws' house for one month, the house they rented in Cambridge, living below the Montgomerys, the faculty apartment on

> campus, and, lastly, the one they own now. One hand, five homes, a lifetime in a fist. (167)

Point of View

The device of the point of view in any literary work gives an internal link to it. In case of *The Namesake*, the author mainly uses the omniscient method of narration, hopping from character to character, place to place and episode to episode with complete freedom and accessing thoughts and feelings of her characters at will. She withholds from Gogol, the knowledge of the reason behind giving him that name, enlightening him only when she feels the fictional narrative demands it. She does not use this method to interpolate her views directly *a la* Fielding or Thackeray. However, she does take liberty in restricting her own freedom and resorts to the third person narrative, whereby she willingly accepts limits to her knowledge of the goings-on in the mind of one character or the other. This "right to intermittent knowledge," as E.M. Forster (88) put it, or the fictional point of view described by Leech and Short as "selective withholding of information, or relinquishing of omniscience" (174) makes the novel more realistic.

The point of view, then, shifts between Gogol and his mother. And even though Lahiri describes Ashima's character with sympathetic insight, it is the male point of view that dominates the narrative. We find it in the description of Gogol-Moushumi relationship as it develops over a period of time:

> He sees her for entire weekends without make-up, sees her with gray shadows under her eyes as she types papers at her desk, and when he kisses her head he tastes the oil that accumulates on her scalp between shampoos. He sees the hair that grows on her legs between waxings, the black roots that emerge between appointments at the salon, and in these moments, these glimpses, he believes he has known no greater intimacy. He learns that she sleeps, always, with her left leg straight and her right leg bent, ankle over knee, in the shape of a 4. He learns that she is prone to snoring, ever so faintly, sounding like a lawn mower that will not start, and

to gnashing her jaws, which he massages for her as she sleeps" (211).

But Moushumi's reaction to Gogol's habits or physique is not given. Even at the end, when Ashima throws a farewell party before leaving for India, it is Gogol who sums it up all:

> Gogol does not know to whom these children belong—half the guests are people his mother has befriended in recent years, people who were at his wedding but whom he does not recognize. People talk of how much they've come to love Ashima's Christmas Eve parties, that they've missed them these past few years, that it won't be the same without her. They have come to rely on her, Gogol realizes. [. . .] In so many ways, his family's life feels like a string of accidents, unforeseen, unintended, one incident begetting another. (286)

Lahiri herself admits that it was basically due to her curiosity about males because she does not have any brother. She was charmed by this dimension and she found it "exhilarating and liberating thing." Her first story 'This Blessed House' which is included in *Interpreter of Maladies,* as also two other stories written thereafter in succession had the male point of view. As she has revealed in an interview given to Subhmoy Das, she always asked herself what a man would think or do in a particular situation. Therefore, even before setting out to write *The Namesake*, she knew that the protagonist of the novel would be a boy.

Language

Lahiri's language is simple and lacks pompousness. It lacks dazzling words that might remain etched in the mind of the reader. She does resort to rhetoric however; which, lined with subtle irony, has the desired effect on the reader:

> Three days later, Ashoke is back at MIT, Alan is back at Harvard, Amber and Clover are back at school. Judy is at work at the collective as usual, and Ashima, on her own with Gogol for the first time in the silent house, suffering from a sleep deprivation far worse than the worst of her jet lag, sits by the three-sided window in the living room on one of the triangular chairs and cries the whole day.

> She cries as she feeds him, and as she pats him to sleep, and as he cries between sleeping and feeding. She cries after the mailman's visit because there are no letters from Calcutta. She cries when she calls Ashoke at his department and he does not answer. One day she cries when she goes to the kitchen to make dinner. (34)

We find brilliant use of grammatical parallelism in the above paragraph. However, Lahiri has missed a wonderful opportunity to explore Ashima's mind here. A stylistic feature of her prose is the fascination for strings of epithets *a la* Charles Lamb's 'Poor Relations': "For being a foreigner, Ashima is beginning to realize is a sort of lifelong pregnancy—a perpetual wait, a constant burden, a continuous feeling out of sorts. It is an ongoing responsibility, a parenthesis in what had once been ordinary life, only to discover that previous life has vanished, replaced by something more complicated and demanding. Like pregnancy, being a foreigner, Ashima believes, is something that elicits the same curiosity from strangers, the same combination of pity and respect" (49-50).

Lahiri has an observant eye. The externals hog better space than the internal details as, for instance, in the following description of Ashoke's attire: "Though Ashima continues to wear nothing but saris and sandals from Bata, Ashoke, accustomed to wearing tailor-made pants and shirts all his life, learns to buy ready-made. He trades in fountain pens or ballpoint pens. [. . .] Though he is now a tenured full professor, he stops wearing jackets and ties to the university. Given that there is a clock everywhere he turns, at the side of his bed, over the stove where he prepares tea, in the car he drives to work, on the wall opposite his desk, he stops wearing a wrist watch, resigning his Favre Leuba to the depths of his sock drawer" (65).

In fact, the novel abounds in descriptive narrative. On the whole, Lahiri's scenic descriptions are fabulous: "He angles his head against the window and watches the autumnal landscape pass: the spewing pink and purple waters of a dye mill, electrical power stations, a big ball-shaped water tank covered with rust. Abandoned factories, with rows of small square windows partly bashed in, ravaged as if by moths. On the trees the topmost branches are bare, the remaining leaves yellow, paper-thin" (120-21).

A careful use of slang and commonplace expressions lends simplicity, ease and freshness of a living language to her style. To be fair to her, however, it must be said that the simplicity of prose does not mean shallowness of ideas. She shows that even economy of language can achieve a rich impact. For that matter, it would be difficult to agree with Sharri Hallgren when he concludes that "simply put [it] does not always equal the deeply felt." In fact, after completing the reading of the novel, one is overwhelmed by the emotions worked up by Lahiri. Hardly there would be any—Ashima, Gogol and Maxine included, who does not win our sympathy. Even the rootless Moushumi appears to us helpless, driven as she is by her raw instincts.

At places, the language degenerates into bland description but even here its aptness and effectiveness cannot be denied:

> Together as the Gangulis drive, they anticipate the moment the thin blue line of ocean will come into view. On the beach Gogol collects rocks, digs tunnels in the sand. He and his father wander barefoot, their pant legs rolled halfway up their calves. He watches his father raise a kite within minutes into the wind, so high that Gogol must tip his head back in order to see, a rippling speck against the sky. Snowy gulls hover with wings spread, low enough to touch. The wind whips around their ears, turning their faces cold. Gogol darts in and out of the ocean, making faint, temporary footprints, soaking his rolled-up cuffs. His mother cries out, laughing, as she lifts her sari a few inches above her ankles, her slippers in one hand, and places her feet in foaming, ice-cold water. (53)

But as a rule, her prose is slightly formal and luminously straightforward. Every sentence reflects honesty and truth. It lacks pretension or pompousness; nor is there any word-play. No less responsible for the verisimilitude is her minute observation that notes every outstanding feature of any situation.

This is as much the story of a Bengali immigrant couple living in America as of their Americanized son Gogol. The atmosphere is sombre and even though the narrative fits in with the atmosphere, an ironic undercurrent of pathos, a kind of self-pity for the brave immigrants, cannot be missed. The *Sunday Telegraph* critic's comment is quite apt: "It is the detail, as much as the ironies embedded in the narrative, that makes *The Namesake* such a joy to read."

The ending of the novel foregrounds language. In the last chapter, Gogol is seen reading the first story in the book *The Short Stories of Nikolai Gogol*. The narrative covering the final one page or so of the novel is noted in future tense: "In a few minutes his mother will come upstairs to find him. 'Gogol,' she will say, opening the door without knocking, 'where is the camera? What's taking so long? This is no time for books,' she will scold, hastily noting the volume open" (290).

The novelist forecasts that Gogol will join the crowded party downstairs, and participate fully, as against his earlier less-than-complete assimilation within the family, and prove thereby his coming of age. But with this limited foray into future, the author shifts back to present and decides to discontinue the story observing simply that Ashima is enjoying the party downstairs while Gogol starts reading the story. The promised moment is left unborn in the womb of future and yet this stylistic twist ends the narrative with a noticeable bang rather than a faint whimper.

The mood after reading the book is indeed grave and contemplative. For that matter, Lahiri has the capability to sentimentalize the narrative even without indulging in rhetoric. The incident in which Ashima leaves her goods intentionally in the train has the economy of narration but it still leaves desired effect. Ashima had knitted a sweater for her father and also purchased some nice paintbrushes as her father was an accomplished illustrator. But when news came of his death, Ashima quietly left the things in the subway train. "As the train slows to a halt she stands, ready to disembark. She does not turn back to look at the shopping bag, left purposely beneath her seat. 'Hey, the Indian lady forgot her stuff,' she hears as the doors shut, and as the train pulls away she hears a fist pounding on glass, but she keeps walking, pushing Gogol along the platform" (46).

Jhumpa Lahiri has a powerful sense of imagery and metaphor. Being a foreigner is likened to "a sort of lifelong pregnancy" (49). Surely, it is no enviable position which anyone, male or female, can easily understand. The train journey justifiably occupies an important place in this diasporic text and it is enriched with metaphors: "The train rattles forward, jostles from side to side, its engine making a sound like the propeller of a plane. The whistle blares intermittently in a minor key. [. . .] Snow covers the straw-coloured ground. Trees stand like spears, dried copper leaves from the previous season still clinging to a few of the branches" (184). The tracks appear as endless ladders here. "For several miles the tracks hug the ocean, which is close enough to touch. The shallowest waves lap against mere inches of shore. He sees a stone bridge, scattered islands the size of rooms, gracious gray and white homes with pleasant views. Boxy houses built on stilts. Lone herons and cormorants perch on bleached wooden posts. Boats with naked masts crowd the marina" (185).

At times, Lahiri breaks into colloquialism but such moments are carefully paced, so that the normal level of a sober language is not disrupted. "A teacher crouches down, one hand holding the newsprint in place, and shows them how" (69). The author resorts to indirect verbatim report of speech thereby conflating the difference between direct speech and indirect report as in the case of Ashima who is waiting to hear from her husband currently in hospital in Cleveland:

> She answers after half a ring, but it's only a telemarketer, some poor soul on weekend duty, asking reluctantly if a Mrs., um—
>
> "Ganguli," Ashima replies tartly before hanging up. (167)

While such an elision of reported speech represents the urgency of the situation, its juxtaposition with direct speech presents a stylistic variation.

Realism in linguistic representation is also borne out by the small smattering of Bengali words used without their English equivalents: *daknam*, *bhalonam*, *sari*, *jamai-to-be*, *mashi*, *pishi*, *maima*, *kaku*, *jethu* etc. Needless to say, it gives authenticity to the text. Lahiri does not quote many native words as another diasporic writer Rohinton Mistry does. Of course, the American spelling of words like caliber, fiber, gangreen and so many others is along expected lines since Jhumpa Lahiri is based in the U.S.A.

Conclusion

The *Sunday Telegraph* rightly commends Jhumpa Lahiri for having "turned a banal trajectory of an unremarkable life to advantage." *The Times* goes a step further and declares that it "spins gold out of the straw of ordinary lives." It is indeed the very common experiences of life of Indian immigrants and their offspring in America that form the staple of this beautiful novel. Lahiri has accomplished the rare feat of sustaining the reader's interest despite a thin plot and ordinary life experiences. Further, the newspaper critic finds "subtle patterns in a string of accidents, unforeseen and unintended." There is no doubt that the novel appears to be episodic and chance plays a very significant role in it. And yet at its root lies the process of maturation of different characters—whether old or young.

The detractors of the novel point to the almost dry prose. "Though Lahiri writes with painstaking care, her dry synoptic style fails to capture the quirkiness of relationships," comments one. (Kakutani). There is no doubt that the language tends to be journalese rather than literary at places but despite this infrequent flaw, one tends to agree with the assessment which acclaims it as "A wonderfully intimate and knowing family portrait...a debut novel that is as assured and eloquent as the work of a longtime master of the craft" (Michiko Kakutani of *New York Times*.)

Chapter 7

The Namesake: Other Important Dimensions

The Title

"What's in a name?"—this rhetorical poser from Shakespeare has become a proverb that suggests the insignificance of name given to objects or people, but Jhumpa Lahiri has, through her novel *The Namesake*, taken it up as a challenge and shown convincingly the importance of a name. The title of the novel itself is indicative of her stand on the issue. Gogol Ganguli is named after the great Russian writer Nikolai Gogol. There is nothing extraordinary about it because a number of people are named after others in this world. It is normal for one to have reverence or fascination for certain historical personalities, even objects of the world or for the sound of plain, abstract words. In case of Jhumpa Lahiri also, her first name 'Jhumpa' was actually her pet name that became good name just like Gogol's. Her good name was supposed to be Nilanjana Swadeshna, which would have been quite an offbeat name even by Indian standards. In an interview, she reveals her fascination for this dual-name system: "I can't speak for all Bengalis. But all the Bengalis I know personally, especially those living in India, have two names, one public, one private. It's always fascinated me" (Das).

In the novel *The Namesake*, however, the name of the protagonist is meant to signify the identity problem that he faces, exposed as he is to twin cultures—American and Indian. In this sense, 'Gogol' must be taken as a metaphor. This name is neither American nor Indian, as the protagonist muses at times. Where could he fit himself in it? How could he relate himself comfortably to a single cultural framework, be it American, Russian or Indian—that was the big problem before him.

The question of belongingness loomed large before him as it must have before his parents when either of them came to America for the first time. Even at the traffic junctions, he found the remnants of his name—GO LEFT, GO RIGHT, GO SLOW etc. but failed to find the complete name which would have provided solace to him. On his visit with his classmates to the cemetery, when other children shriek with joy over having come across gravestones mentioning American names, he knows there would be no 'Ganguli' here. His moorings are not in America, nor will his body occupy any piece of land here, because after his death, his body will be burnt. His is a strange name here as the chaperone accompanying the children tells him, comparing the strangeness of old names to that of his own name. His own sister Sonia also could not accept this name without murmur and oftentimes called him 'Goggles.' His class mates would tease him by calling him 'Goggle' or 'Gargle.' Still worse was the ugly word-play enacted by some ruffians when they overwrote 'green' on 'guli' turning the family surname into 'Gangreen'—the name of a hateful disease.

His father had been impressed by the writer Nikolai Gogol. He could relate to him because the author was the favourite of his grandfather also and in this way, he felt a sense of belongingness, for he had been his grandpa's blue-eyed boy who read to him the stories in the former's old age. Now that he was an immigrant in America, Ashoke still found affinity with Nikolai Gogol as he also had spent all his life in exile. Ashoke's favourite story in the book *The Short Stories of Nikolai Gogol* was 'The Overcoat.' This was the story he had been reading when the train accident occurred. This story is about one Akaky Akakyevich, who passed his life time copying documents written by others and suffering insults from others. Ashoke found in him the image of his father who was also a clerk

His story 'The Overcoat' was taken up in Gogol's class and Gogol simplified the story of the great writer thus: "There was hardly anything remarkable about this life. Gogol Ganguli failed to find any connection with the great writer the way his father had. There was nothing original about Akaky's work as he passed his days copying documents written by others only. It symbolized a life not quite one's own. Was Gogol also leading someone else's (Nikolai's) life? This is what horrified him.

He tried to forget this name as he felt that he was not living his authentic life under the name of his namesake. After he had turned major and applied for admission to the Yale University, he undertook the proper legal procedure for adopting another name—Nikhil. He was now immensely satisfied that he had finally done something original on his own and buried the problematic identity attached to that name. His friends and new class mates at the Yale called him Nikhil now. His parents—Ashoke and Ashima—started using this name whenever they talked with his roommates on phone. This upset him for it meant a certain loss—that of his pet name and signified changed relationship—a formal one, with his parents. Any loss takes its own time to sink in.

Later, his father told him about the mystery behind his name—the train accident and his rescue, courtesy the sole page of the book shaking meekly in his hand. Gogol had felt sorry for his attitude towards the name given by his father. He was apologetic about his earlier reaction. At the same time, his initial anger at not having been made privy to the secret earlier was overtaken by sympathy for his father. He felt related to his father.

He remained Gogol for his parents at home and he had no objection to it; rather he liked it, for it connected him to the family in the Indian way. For the world, however, it could not be possible for him to "reinvent himself fully, to break from the mismatched name." Thus, he partook of the Indian identity and heritage through the name and found implicit security in it. Despite his American environs, he had come to absorb nuances of Indian culture which became evident when he gave up Maxine for the sake of his mother.

But then, when Moushumi inadvertently revealed the episode of his name-change to a gathering of friends at the Astrid's party, he felt humiliated beyond words. The perpetrator of the crime was his own wife to whom he had told the secret with the rider that he least desired to be reminded of it because in that case his mind would go back to the near-fatal train accident involving his father. It was breach of trust on the part of his life partner which he took seriously.

Jhumpa Lahiri has also highlighted the importance of the name through a contrast in the novel. Gogol was shaken when he heard Dimitri's name from the lips of his wife. "For the first time in his life, another man's name had upset Gogol more than his own" (283). He contrasts it with the state of his mind at the time of revelation by his father of the train accident and the importance of Nikolai Gogol's name in his life. "That night he'd experienced the same bewilderment, was sickened in the same way. But he had felt none of the tenderness that he had felt for his father, only anger, the humiliation of having been deceived" (282).

After the death of his father, when his mother planned to divide her time between India and America, Gogol is upset again, for he realizes nobody would call him Gogol now. In the end, Gogol goes back to the story 'The Overcoat' written by his namesake Nikolai Gogol and finds what he has not so far: "Born March 20, 1809. The death of his father, 1825. Publishes his first story, 1830. Travels to Rome, 1837. Dies 1852, one month before his forty-third birthday" (289). This chronology of the author makes him reflect on his own life. He is younger than the author by ten years, so in another ten years, he will be of that age when the latter died.

He wonders if he will be married again and have a child whose name would be given by him. He will begin a new job at a smaller architectural firm where he will produce his own designs. He has hopes of becoming an associate of the firm and seeing his name 'Nikhil' incorporated in the firm. The name 'Gogol,' which was purposely hidden and legally diminished, has no chance of survival. That will be the end of the dilemma involving the name 'Gogol.' He will not be bothered about clarifying the reference to his namesake—the great Russian writer Nikolai Gogol. This should be a matter of satisfaction to him.

Autobiographical Element

Jhumpa Lahiri wrote the novel *The Namesake*, some four years after she had brought out her collection of short stories titled *Interpreter of Maladies*. It is quite common for a writer to depend upon his actual experience of life when he starts writing a work of fiction. But whereas her first work suggests inspiration from the Indian diasporic community of America, the novel bears a clear stamp of autobiography. Starting from the details of life in Calcutta to the identity problem of the second generation of immigrants in America, there are several aspects which are based on Lahiri's own life experiences.

She clearly states that when she started writing fiction, her stories had Calcutta as their locale. Although she was born in England and brought up in America, she had been going to Calcutta in the company of her family which made periodic visits to that city. In her novel *The Namesake*, the Gangulis do undertake visits to Calcutta after regular intervals. There is no doubt that "these trips, to a vast, unruly fascinating city so different from the small New England town" where she had been raised shaped her perception of the world, which had that "necessary combination of distance and intimacy" so very essential for a meaningful engagement of a writer with her story.

Even for the name of the protagonist of the novel, Lahiri is obliged to her Indian roots, as she admits in an interview, "The original spark of the book was the fact that a friend of my cousin's in India had the pet name Gogol. I wanted to write about the pet name / good name distinction for a long time, and I knew I needed the space of a novel to explore the idea. It's almost too perfect a metaphor for the experience of growing up as the child of immigrants, having a divided identity, divided loyalties, etc." (Das)

So, even while living in America throughout, India has always formed part of her fictional landscape and her characters have an Indian background. India keeps cropping up as a setting, sometimes literally, sometimes more figuratively, in the memory of the characters. *The Namesake* is, essentially, a story of the life of Indian immigrants in the United States, so the American setting was bound to be there. "The terrain is very much the terrain of my own life—New England and New York, with Calcutta always hovering in the background. Now that the writing is done I've realized that America is a real presence in the book; the characters must struggle and come to terms with what it means to live here, to be brought up here, to belong and not belong here" she says.

With the passage of time, she feels that she has inherited "a sense of exile" from her parents even though in many ways she is more American than them. "In fact," she says, "it is still very hard to think of myself as an American. (This is of course complicated by the fact that I was born in London.) I think that for immigrants, the challenges of exile, the loneliness, the constant sense of alienation, the knowledge of and longing for a lost world, are more explicit and distressing than for their children. On the other hand, the problem for the children of immigrants—those with strong ties to their country of origin—is that they feel neither one thing nor the other. This has been my experience, in any case. For example, I never know how to answer the question "Where are you from?" If I say I'm from Rhode Island, people are seldom satisfied. They want to know more, based on things such as my name, my appearance, etc. Alternatively, if I say I'm from India, a place where I was not born and have never lived, this is also inaccurate. It bothers me less now. But it bothered me growing up, the feeling that there was no single place to which I fully belonged."

The postmodernist that Jhumpa is, to her the issue of belonging is ultimately a question of allegiance, of choice. Like a dutiful child, she always wanted to please her parents and meet their expectations. Besides, she also wanted to meet the expectations of her American peers, as also her own expectation of fitting into the American society. It was a classic case of divided identity, but depending on the degree to which the immigrants in question are willing to assimilate, the conflict does come up in the lives of the immigrants.

In fact, Jhumpa's parents were fearful and suspicious of America and American culture when she was growing up. Maintaining ties with India, and preserving Indian traditions in America, meant a lot to them. Later, they felt more at home, but it does not mean that the problem of owing allegiance to a single culture has been resolved. They will "always feel like, and be treated as, foreigners here," according to her. Lahiri is mature enough to understand the position. She, therefore, understands and sympathizes with her parents' predicament.

When Jhumpa was a child it was harder for her to understand their views. At times she felt that their expectations for her were in direct opposition to the reality of the world in which they lived. Things like dating, living on one's own, having close friendships with Americans, listening to American music and eating American food were not appreciated by them. It was not until she was in college that her American friends expressed curiosity about and interest in her Indian background. As a young child, she says, she felt like having two identities in which the Indian part of her was unacknowledged, by her American environment. "I felt that I led two very separate lives," she says.

It is quite common for Indians—Bengalis and others to have two names—one public and the other private. Lahiri admits that this has always attracted her:

> My parents are called by different names depending on what country they happen to be in; in India they're known by their pet names, but in America they're known by their good names. My sister, who was born and raised in America, has two names. I'm like Gogol in that my pet name inadvertently became my good name. I have two other names on my passport and my birth certificate (my mother couldn't settle on just one). But when I was enrolled in school the teachers decided that Jhumpa was the easiest of my names to pronounce and that was that. To this day many of my relatives think that it's both odd and inappropriate that I'm known as Jhumpa in an official, public context" (Das).

Clearly, the character Gogol crafted by her is her alter ego even in the minute context of identity-crisis arising out of name.

Lahiri clarifies that she does not feel connected to Nikolai Gogol, the Russian writer. He is not her inspiration at least with regard to language or characterization. She also draws distinction between her language and that used by Gogol. "His writing is more overtly comic, more antic and absurd than mine tends to be," but she did read his writings when she adopted his name for her own character in the novel *The Namesake*. She liked the story 'The Overcoat' which is an important point of reference in her novel. "It really does haunt me the way it haunts the character of Ashoke in the novel. I like to think that every writer I admire influences me in some way, by teaching me something about writing. Of course, without the inspiration of Nikolai Gogol, without his name and without his writing, my novel would never have been conceived. In that respect, this book came out of Gogol's overcoat, quite literally" (Das), she says.

Realism

Jhumpa Lahiri in her debut novel *The Namesake* weaves a story covering three decades of the Ganguli household in the USA with fine-tuned sensibility that combines realism—social and psychological. This realism conveyed in succinct prose is indeed an outstanding feature of this promising novelist who has already made a mark in the literary world, winning Man Booker for her first fictional work. There is nothing fanciful or fantastic about the portrayal of society. Similarly, at the individual level, the characters portrayed are psychologically convincing.

The eight-month long stay of the Ganguli family in India is described in the fourth chapter of the novel, in which she delves deep into life in India and notes "the short, dark men pulling rickshaws and the crumbling buildings side by side with fretwork balconies, hammers and sickles painted on their facades. He [Gogol] stares at the commuters clinging precariously to trains and buses, threatening at any moment to spill onto the street rickshaws on roads, and at the families who boil rice and shampoo their hair on the sidewalk" (82).

On their visit to India, they also learn about the bandits who loot passengers travelling in trains, so that when they go sightseeing to Agra, Ashoke carries cash hidden in the pocket of a special garment under the shirt and Ashima and Sonia remove their gold jewels beforehand. Nothing happens on the outward journey, but on their way back, they learn that a businessman in another compartment was stabbed and robbed of three lac rupees. They also fall ill when they reach back Calcutta.

Lahiri's faculty of minute observation makes the depiction of even ordinary situations quite realistic. As an example, we may refer to the scene in which the Gangulis return to America after spending eight months in India:

> Within twenty-four hours he and his family are back on Pemberton Road, the late August grass in need of trimming, a quart of milk and some bread left by their tenants in the refrigerator, four grocery bags on the staircase filled with mail. At first the Gangulis sleep most of the day and are wide awake at night, gorging themselves on toast at three in the morning, unpacking the suitcases one by one. Though they are home they are disconcerted by the space, by the uncompromising silence that surrounds them. They still feel somehow in transit, still disconnected from their lives, bound up in an alternate schedule, an intimacy only the four of them share. But by the end of the week, after his mother's friends come to admire her new gold and saris, after the eight suitcases have been aired out on the sundeck and put away, after the chanachur is poured into Tupperware and the smuggled mangoes eaten for breakfast with cereal and tea, it's as if they've never been gone. (87)

She concerns herself with the educated middle class Indians in America. Her portrayal of the party circuit involving Moushumi and Gogol reminds one of Jane Austen who deals with subjects like marriage, child-birth, relatives, parties etc. in her novel *Emma*. Lahiri's scenes are mostly laid in restaurants and drawing rooms. But of course, she does not have Austen's essential moral approach towards social attitude and behaviour. She only faithfully portrays individuals and society in their true colours.

Her realism banks, to a great extent, on the variety of names of objects—mostly of eatables. We are introduced to some French dishes and drinks which Gogol savours in the company of Moushumi Mazoomdar: "She orders a salad and the bouillabaisse and a bottle of Sancerre. He orders the cassoulet. [. . .] They order espresso and share a crème brulee" (198). When they meet a week later at an Italian restaurant, the writer has the opportunity to display her knowledge of Italian dishes and liquor. They enjoyed pasta, porcini ravioli and a salad of arugula and pears washed down with two glasses of merlot. At her own apartment, she serves him olives and "some goat cheese coated with ash" (208). She is planning to prepare "coq au vin" with the help of a cookbook. (209) They throw parties for their friends at which they play "bossa nova and serve bread and salami and cheese" (228).

In addition to the class names of objects, we also find brand names which further add to the authenticity of detail. The description of things in Moushumi's room supports this view: "a Kashmiri crewelwork carpet on the floor, Rajasthani silk pillows on the sofa, a cast-iron Natraj on one of the bookcases" (208). When Gogol and Moushumi settle down after their marriage in one-room apartment in New York, they shop for various items of furniture and furnishings: "Imitation Noguchi lamps, a black sectional sofa, kilim and flokati carpets, a blond wood platform bed" (228).

The surfeit of brand names also points to the consumerist culture of America. Moushumi occasionally visits a store named Bendel's on the Fifth Avenue in New York to buy her make-up. She goes to a cinema named 'Paris' to see an old movie and to the Plaza to have drinks. The brand name may be joined to class nouns for an effective appeal. So, she finds the shoes arranged in a shoe-shop on Lucite pedestal "glowing under a spot-light, the gladiator-style straps festooned with rhinestones" (249). All through, there is an attempt to be mathematically precise. This is a general trait of her prose which bears the stamp of journalese rather than of classical literary language.

Realism also comes from having a minor detail as an add-on to a major action, as in the restaurant scene in New York where Nikhil and Moushumi go on the recommendation of Donald and Astrid but where she hardly enjoys the meals or the service. As they get up to leave, a waiter hands over Moushumi's pashmina shawl to her which had fallen on the floor. She notices that her black dress is coated with lilac fibres. She tries to remove them but in vain. Nikhil asks as to what the matter is to which she says "Nothing" (252). They leave finally. This small incident is dispensable and yet its mention makes the scene more real, for there need not always be clean entrances and exits.

According to Sukhdev Sindhu of the *Daily Telegraph*, "Lahiri's prose is striking. Spurning the transcultural wordplay of many Asian-American authors, she writes with journalistic precision. Like a Victorian urban chronicler, she loves to amass inventories. Things matter to her and to her characters; they are bulwarks against drift and confusion."

R.W. Desai finds stereotyping of Indian lifestyle in the novel, done primarily with an eye on the American book market. To him, the revelation by Gogol of the absence of public display of love by his parents smacks of Jhumpa Lahiri's attempt to cater to the western expectation of rigidity among Indians on this score. Had it been a key element in the novelist's repertoire, such an attack would have been justified but as it is, there is only a brief reference to this aspect of Indian life against a host of other comparisons. This detail should be juxtaposed with Lahiri's mention of the disorder and mess in the house of her landlord Prof. Montgomery which Ashima finds offensive to her Indian sense of purity and cleanliness. Even so, Lahiri presents it matter-of-factly and does not pass any judgmental comment on it. No one can deny that it is a reality and a novelist is expected to be realistic in his approach.

Humour

Humour is intentionally included in the narrative by some of the best novelists so that the interest of the reader is retained. In fact, a lengthy novel does need it otherwise an average reader finds it difficult to stick to it. Even in Thomas Hardy, one finds the sobriety of the narrative punctuated at places, howsoever fewer, by brief humorous descriptions. In Indian English fiction, Rohinton Mistry has included a number of jokes in his novel *Such a Long Journey*. These are mouthed by his characters Dinshawji and Gustad Noble while passing their lunch hour in the canteen. Some novelists are gifted with the rare gift of creating laughter through subtle irony of description or situation.

The novel *The Namesake* revolves around the identity of Gogol and his name has a lot to do with it. This, by itself, is an amusing motif. However, the humour in this novel is subdued. There are few places where we have explicit humour. Mostly, humour is created through situation like the several awkwardly-handled love affairs of Gogol and Moushumi. Of course, the out-of-proportion blowing of the problem due to Gogol's twin names—*daknam* and *bhalonam* takes the cake. The dialogues are few and far between and are mostly business-like and are, therefore, devoid of humour. But there are some very fine instances of humorous description.

When it comes to naming the newborn, the Gangulis decide upon Ashima's grandmother to "do the honours"! In India, the elders in the family are respected and seeking their guidance in such a matter is considered to be obligatory on the younger people. But considering the fact that the Gangulis were immigrants in an alien environment where their innocent reverence for the matriarch would only arouse giggles, they could have avoided such a course. "In India, parents take their time. It wasn't unusual for years to pass before the right name, the best possible name, was determined. Ashima and Ashoke can both cite examples of cousins who were not officially named until they were registered, at six or seven, in school" (25). For any American reader, these nuggets of wisdom would definitely come as ticklers.

From this point starts a kind of conflict between the pet name or *daknam* and the name proper or *bhalonam* (Bengali for 'good name'). Now, it is quite common to hear people ask "Your good name, sir?," but the Americans do not discriminate between names as 'good' or 'bad.' For the western reader, this tussle is bound to arouse guffaws of laughter. The writer devotes considerable lines to enlighten the reader about the importance of the issue: "Every pet name is paired with a good name, a *bhalonam*, for identification in the outside world. Consequently, good names appear on envelopes, on diplomas, in telephone directories and in all other public places. (For this reason, letters from Ashima's mother say 'Ashima' on the outside, 'Monu' on the inside.)" (26). While the name 'Ashoke' refers to the great Indian emperor, the writer humorously comments, "Pet names have no such aspirations"! (26) This dual name problem is encountered by the Gangulis at the time of Gogol's admission to the elementary school where the Principal is not able to understand the difference between a good name and the one used at home. Gogol is found dumbstruck when he is addressed as Nikhil and asked questions. So, the Principal, going by the child's preference, enters Gogol in the record. (58) At school, Gogol's hatred for his name has grown so much that "The sight of it printed in capital letters on the crinkly page upsets him viscerally." (89).

When the Gangulis move to their own house—a shingled two-story colonial erected on a quarter acre of land, they discover "how much they possess; each of them had come to America with a single suitcase, a few weeks' worth of clothes. Now there are enough old issues of the *Globe* stacked in the corners of the apartment to wrap all their plates and glasses. There are whole years of *Time* magazine to toss out." (51) This kind of assessment of their wealth is bound to create laughter.

Here is a brilliant example of Lahiri's humorous style. For once, no holds barred: "Mr. Lawson is a slight, wiry *shamelessly preppy* man with a *surprisingly* deep voice, reddish blond hair, smallish but penetrating green eyes, horn-rimmed glasses. He is the subject of *schoolwide speculation, and slight scandal*, having once been married to Ms. Sagan, who teaches French. He wears khakis and Shetland sweaters in bright solid colors, Kelly green and yellow and red, sips black coffee continually from the *same chipped blue mug, cannot survive* the fifty-minute class without excusing himself to go to the teachers' lounge for a cigarette. *In spite of his diminutive stature* he has a commanding, captivating presence in the room. His handwriting is *famously illegible*; student compositions are regularly returned *stamped with tan rings of coffee, sometimes golden rings of Scotch*" (88; italics mine).

Needless to say, the description is bound to send one into spasms of boisterous laughter.

The traditional mindset of Bengalis in the matter of marriage of girls provides an occasion to Jhumpa Lahiri to let loose her satiric shafts dipped in irony: "From the onset of adolescence she'd been subjected to a series of unsuccessful schemes; every so often a small group of unmarried Bengali men materialized in the house, young colleagues of her father's. [. . .] During summer visits to Calcutta, strange men mysteriously appeared in the sitting room of her grandparents' flat" (213). The undercurrent of subtle humour in these lines cannot be missed.

Jhumpa Lahiri can imbue even a small phrase with powerful humour. While working in Paris, Moushumi is reported to have fallen in love with Graham, an investment banker from New York who was living in Paris. For his sake, she joined the New York University. Both of them lived in New York, without letting their families know. When her parents came to visit her, he would disappear to a hotel "removing all traces of himself from the apartment" (216). Again, when Moushumi is involved with Gogol, the intimacy between them deepens so much that within six months "they have clothes and toothbrushes at each other's apartments" (211). Clearly, the understatement arouses laughter here.

At a party thrown by Moushumi's friends Donald and Astrid at their Brooklyn home, the party talk centres around naming of children. One of the guests, Colin says that he likes names that signify a virtue, like Patience, Faith, Chastity etc. His great-grandmother, he says, was named 'Silence' "something nobody wants to believe" (243). The climax to the discussion is provided by Gogol when he says that there is no such thing as a perfect name. His suggestion is that human beings should be allowed to name themselves when they turn eighteen. Until then, he says, pronouns could be used in place of names!

Even after her marriage, Moushumi does not wish to forgo her life as a single individual. On the pretext of studying, she has been indulging in innocent activities of her choice like going for a walk by herself or seeing Astrid and her baby. She wants to reassure herself that she could still be independent. The writer has a tongue-in-cheek explanation for her behaviour: "Along with the Sanskrit vows she'd repeated at her wedding, she'd privately vowed that she'd never grow fully dependent on her husband, as her mother has!" (247). These instances, indeed not many, are a reliable indicator of the author's capability to make the narrative lively and interesting.

Ending of the Novel

While some young readers complain of a tepid ending—something not expected of a popular novel which it certainly is, a maturer reader is very likely to be satisfied with it, for it winds up a significant portion—the period of youth and middle age—of Ashima's life. Ashoke died in between and the children are on their own now. While Sonia is blissfully married, Gogol has matured, tasted the fruit of marriage and moved on in life. His initial problem with his name has been solved after his father's death. The sentiments behind the name are now appreciated by him, not because he has been impressed by any logic but by another overriding sentiment that connects an estranged son to his father. Unfortunately, it happens after Ashoke's death. And in this linkage, no cultural barrier comes in between. Death is a universal fact and the feelings associated with it are also universal. No loss is greater than the loss of one's close relative. So, the apparent barriers erected between father and son by Gogol's upbringing in American milieu and his feeble Indian acculturation are not potent enough to stand up to the human sentiments of which both the parents and the children partake.

Therefore, when Gogol goes to see off his mother who is proceeding to India, he wonders how his parents had managed to leave their families behind in India, seeing them so infrequently "dwelling unconnected, in a perpetual state of expectation, of longing" (281). Whenever he happened to go along with his parents to Calcutta, he never really enjoyed it and perhaps nursed a secret grudge against his parents for going there too often, but now he feels differently: "All those trips to Calcutta he'd once resented—how could they have been enough? They were not enough" (281).

Gogol realizes that his parents lived in America "in spite of what was missing" and now that he seems to be facing the same prospect of missing his only parent alive, he feels he lacks the stamina for it. Gogol is the one who had a troubled relationship not only with his girl friends, but also with his parents on account of his name as also on account of the culture and generation gap. But at the end of the novel, there is indication of his understanding his parents' position. Even though he had stayed deliberately away from his parents, yet he hovered close enough to his house. Only when his father moved to Cleveland, was he a little more distant from him. He realizes that he came home for the sake of his family only. That means he was unconsciously tied to his family even as he interiorized the ways of the peer group—the American youth. It is the repressed part of his consciousness that shows itself now. Along with the physical part, the emotional part of his self seems to have been inherited from his Indian parents. It is no less than a revelation to him.

Ashima, the only surviving parent, understands why her children acted the way they did. She no longer wonders at their falling in love first and then taking a long time to get married, something far more different than the single afternoon which was taken by Ashoke and Ashima to get married. Even though she had refused for many years to accept life in America, she knows that this is "home nevertheless—the world for which she is responsible, which she has created, which is everywhere around her, needing to be packed up, given away, thrown out bit by bit" (280).

There is another way to look at the family life, Gogol thinks. It has been "a string of accidents, unforeseen, unintended, one incident begetting another" (286). It all started with his father's train accident. The name chosen for him by his great-grandmother was lost and so he got his name Gogol. He tried to correct the randomness and irrelevance of the name, but he could not free him from this bondage and "re-invent himself fully." His marriage was a wrong step and then his father's death was the worst accident. "And yet these events have formed Gogol, shaped him, determined who he is. They were things for which it was impossible to prepare but which one spent a lifetime looking back at, trying to accept, interpret, comprehend. Things that should never have happened, that seemed out of place and wrong, these were what prevailed, what endured, in the end" (287). Finally, when Gogol gets hold of the book *The Short Stories of Nikolai Gogol* in the bedroom of his late father in the final chapter of the novel, he regards it as another accident.

In the last chapter, Ashima is seen preparing for a party prior to her taking up a roving life, thirty two years after reaching America. She will be leaving Pemberton Road house where she has lived for twenty-seven years—a duration longer than any spent elsewhere in America. She intends spending six months in India and the remaining six in the U.S.A. She would be truly 'without borders' now, true to the meaning of her name 'Ashima.'

The guests start pouring in at seven-thirty and the party starts. They recall the Christmas celebrations held earlier on the Pemberton Road when Ashoke was alive. Now they would miss these parties. Ashima asks Gogol to bring the camera and get some photographs. He goes upstairs to get his father's Nikon camera. There are so many things lying there, out of which he picks up a book—*The Short Stories of Nikolai Gogol*—which had been presented on his birthday by his father. It still bears the inscription: "For Gogol Gangulī" and alongside are the words in his father's hand: "The man who gave you his name, from the man who gave you your name" (288). His father's handwriting reminds him of the cheques that his father used to send him throughout his career as a college student. Gogol realizes that after his mother is gone, the name Gogol Ganguli would vanish from the lips of his loved ones and so, "cease to exist" (289). Surprisingly, this is disconcerting rather than reassuring for him. After all, he had yearned fiercely to shed this name!

Gogol now compares the life of Nikolai Gogol with his own. After a month, he would be starting on a new job producing his own designs and it is very likely that he would become an associate of the firm and his name Nikhil would be incorporated in the firm's name. Thus, whereas the name Gogol was purposely hidden, Nikhil would live on. He starts reading the first story. The rest of the story contained in the final one page or so of the novel is noted in future tense. The writer says that in a few minutes his mother will come upstairs to find him and ask him about the camera. Looking at the books strewn on the bed, she will disapprove of his reading at this hour when the party is in progress downstairs. The writer says Gogol will apologize and go down with his mother and be witness to what had been the usual party scene when his father was alive.

But then Lahiri gives up the future tense and shifts to the present, saying that Gogol is happy to have recovered the book which would otherwise have been lost. He continues reading the book. The writer, who became a crystal gazer a short while ago, discards her epiphany to the world of probability and instead chooses to enter the mind of her creation Ashima and discovers latter's ignorance of what Gogol is engrossed in, upstairs. This collocation of the fictional point of view with the omniscient narrative is again a uniqueness of her art that gives a momentary surprise to the readers just before they have laid the novel down.

Film Version of the Novel

A number of stories and novels dealing with the diasporic condition have been produced by writers of Indian origin belonging to the first or second generation of immigrants. While turning a novel into a film, some changes have to be made of necessity, because of the difference of medium. It depends upon the director of the film as to which changes he thinks will render the film livelier and more entertaining. To be commercially viable, a film must appeal to a wider cross-section of society than the one that accesses the novel format. Mira Nair, who has adapted the novel *The Namesake* for a film of the same title, is a celebrated film director. She too belongs to the Indian diaspora settled in America and therefore, has some ground for affinity with the writer of the novel.

The film starts with the platform scene and is quickly followed by the train crash in which Ashoke gets badly injured. This is a departure from the novel where this accident is related in the form of Ashoke's flashback while he is waiting in the hospital where his wife is admitted for child-birth. The change of sequence makes the opening scene laid in India of considerable interest to the foreign viewer while the Indian audience can easily relate to it. The characters of Indian origin speak English with a marked Indian accent whereas the second generation born and brought up in America has the standard American accent—something that goes along with the realistic treatment for which Mira Nair is known.

In order to make the film more focussed and to compress it within the time span, without attenuating the impact on the audience, some scenes have been amputated, as for example, Gogol's affair with Ruth. Similarly, the somewhat lengthy scene covering Moushumi with a cigarette dangling from her fingers remains etched in the mind of the viewer and underlines the unconventional image of an Americanized child of Indian immigrants. Mira Nair's films are known for their realistic portrayal. She is not given to undue sentimentalization so much so that even when there is occasion like heart-to-heart talk between estranged lovers, Nair allows little time for the already frugal dialogues of the novel.

It is a fact that novel-writing and film-making are separate areas and rather than considering a filmmaker as only a translator, he/she should be seen as a creator. While reading a fictional work, the reader or a film-maker employs his/her own imagination to recreate on the mental or the celluloid screen what the novel intends to convey. While reading *The Namesake* in the movie format, we have to deal with the film-maker as the mediating agency. The film-maker may give the story a twist and indeed, Mira Nair has done so here.

There is no doubt that while adapting the novel for the film, Mira Nair has changed the focus from the character Gogol to the Ganguli family affairs. Whereas Lahiri chose the title of the novel with the identity problem of the second generation Indian-

American in mind, Nair seems to have been motivated by the current American concerns about family as a sociological unit—something that hogs the limelight even in the election speeches during Presidential elections in America. However, Nair, while speaking in the context of Lahiri's latest collection of short stories, relates this shifting of focus to her own interest in the institution of family: "When I was working on the stories in *Unaccustomed Earth*, I did have a moment of feeling very aware and also kind of excited by the realization that I seemed to be writing a lot about families and family dynamics" (Owens).

So far as the revelation of American ambience and culture is concerned, Nair's film has been immensely successful. The lead cast, including Imran Khan and Tabu, has impressively played their parts as Indians planted on the American soil. Kal Penn plays the young Gogol. Jhumpa Lahiri has also made a cameo appearance as Aunt Jhumpa in the film. The Ganguli couple has not been Americanized the way their children have been. Their accent is Indian as is Ashima's dress. On the whole, the director has been successful in bringing out the disconnect that the first generation immigrants from India feel vis-à-vis America and that felt by the second generation of these immigrants with regard to India. The in-betweenness is a necessary condition even as the second generation is better placed in terms of age to fit into the American milieu.

The film version has received mixed response as the following comment would signify: "Due to its resonant base, Nair's *The Namesake* is indeed 'another work of art' (Wagner), but does not intend to efface the cultural memory of the novel (Ellis) [. . .]. In fact, the uniqueness of the original text (Lahiri's) is further illuminated by the cinematic refraction of the original (Pellow). Not just a 'picture book' (Orr) or a 'shrunken version of the novel, a précis of sorts, Nair's film is a superlative 'critical commentary' (Pellow)" (Shrivastava 42-43).

Cross-Cultural Tensions in *The Namesake*: An America-born Indian's Search for Identity

SANTWANA HALDAR
Balasore

Cross-cultural conflicts—confrontations giving rise to socio-psychological theories as well as alliances leading to survival and development—are, naturally, the focal point in the works of the immigrant writers. Chaman Nahal says, "Maybe two large segments of cultures such as the East and the West cannot meet in harmony; some of us believe they can. All right, they meet in disharmony. It is all the same a meeting, a meeting of meanings."[1] After becoming a U.S. citizen in 1988, Bharati Mukherjee writes, "I was a psychological expatriate though a naturalized Canadian for fifteen years simply because Canada is a country officially hostile to the concept of assimilation. Perceiving myself to be in a comfortable but unwelcoming environment, I struggled to maintain various emblems of my difference."[2] Bapsi Sidhwa confesses the nature of the problem faced by immigrant writers: "Of course, it is not easy to portray the nuances of a culture one is not born to, and it entails a risk to get inside the shin of a character that is shaped by another culture."[3] Jhumpa Lahiri admits, "It [America] is home to me but [I] feel a bit of an outsider too."[4] While Lahiri's short stories in *Interpreter of Maladies* (Pulitzer Prize Winner, 2000) give us a glimpse into the lives of the Indians in exile, "navigating between the strict traditions they've inherited and the baffling New World they must encounter everyday" (Introductory note of *Interpreter of Maladies*), her first full-length novel *The Namesake* successfully deals not only with issues of different cultures and the sufferings of the new immigrants, but also with the identity crisis of the second generation immigrants, who have no intention to be linked with India in any way, but fail to become hundred percent Americans in their approaches to life. This article centres on the latent sufferings of its central character Gogol whose loneliness owes much, if not directly, to his parents' roots in India.

The Namesake starts with Ashima Ganguli, a Calcutta-bred woman married to Ashoke, a doctoral candidate in electrical engineering at MIT, who is trying hard to get herself adjusted to a Central Square apartment in Cambridge where she finds hardly anything that looks similar with the thing she has been acquainted with in West Bengal, India. The process of adjustment is all the more difficult with her first pregnancy, when she is put in the labour room of a hospital; when she goes back to their apartment with the baby boy, she is horrified with the thought of bringing up the baby all alone in that foreign country. Lahiri reveals the tit-bits of her struggle—her success in bringing up a son and a daughter, her friendship with other Bengali couples in USA, her role as a perfect partner of a scientist-cum-professor and her calm decision to sell her apartment and go back to India after the sudden death of her husband. "For being a foreigner, Ashima is beginning to realize, is a sort of lifelong pregnancy—a perpetual wait, a constant burden, a continuous feeling out of sorts. It is an ongoing responsibility, a parenthesis in what had once been ordinary life, only to discover that previous life has vanished, replaced by something more complicated and demanding" (49-50). But as the plot of the novel advances, Ashima's struggle goes in the background of the story at the centre of which comes her son who struggles secretly to fight the hurdles imposed on him. The first hurdle faced by him is his name. It is almost mysterious that the letter containing the good name of Ashima's son sent by her grandmother, who kept the name a secret to others, was missing and the name suggested by her could never be known because of her sudden death following a coma stage.

Thanks to the paraphernalia in the offices of the States, the baby had to be given a name immediately and Ashoke suggested the name 'Gogol,' the last name of the Russian writer Nikolai Gogol, who was his favourite author in his school days. During a night trip to Jamshedpur from Calcutta, Ashoke was engrossed in the stories of Gogol when the train had an accident killing almost all the passengers of the compartment. He was miraculously saved however, though injured badly; when he was rescued, he still held Gogol's book in his hand and this incident prompted him to believe that the writer was somehow responsible for his survival. This incident was the cause behind naming his son after that great writer, though he thought of it to be a nickname only. But the nickname continued to be the good name as well: when Ashoke tried to replace Gogol with Nikhil at the time of getting the son admitted in school, the boy did not respond to the new name and the principal liked to keep the name Gogol in the school register, without bothering about the parents' preference to the new name. The fear of the little boy when he is admitted to the kindergarten is expressed in a unique way: "He is afraid to be Nikhil, someone he does not know. Who does not know him" (57). Gradually, the name Gogol is associated with his childhood, with the time when he along with his sister Sonia enjoyed the local rituals having no other feeling but a sense of belonging to the land. At the same time he was forced to mix with his parents' Bengali friends and to get acquainted with Bengali culture against his will, and developed a mixed feeling that stood on the way of his feeling like a son of the soil.

One day when he was taken to cemeteries on a field trip arranged by the school, the peculiarity of his name becomes apparent. He is old enough to know by that time that there is no Ganguli among the names of the dead who are buried there, that "his body will occupy no plot of earth, that no stone in this country will bear his name beyond life" (69). Yet he has not been much aware of his identity as an immigrant in America. While recording the names of the dead in the cemetery—he likes those names, their oddities, their flamboyance—he hears a comment of one of the chaperones that those names are not heard these days, as are his own name. Gogol is suddenly aware of names that "die over time," that "they perish just as people do" (70).

Back home, he keeps the rubbings he has brought from the cemetery though his mother asks him to throw them away. "For reasons he cannot explain or necessarily understand, these ancient Puritan spirits, these very first immigrants to America, these bearers of unthinkable, obsolete names, have spoken to him, so much so that in spite of his mother's disgust he refuses to throw the rubbings away" (71). From this time on Gogol begins to suffer from a sense of insecurity, one that prompts him to come out of the immigrant's feeling nurtured by his parents who never forget their identity as Indians and even try to impose that identity on their children.[5]

Gogol has already begun to hate his name as he finds that students tease him saying "giggle" or "gargle," that substitute-teachers at school always pause when they arrive at his name on the roster, that his classmates shout "Go, Gogle" on golden autumn days as he runs the bases. His ears burn when he discovers that the word Ganguli in their mailbox has been shortened to gang, with the word 'green' scrawled in pencil following it. He runs back into the house, sickened, certain of the insult his father will feel. He feels that the insult is intended for his parents whose accents, he has noted, are smirked at in stores. But his father is unaffected, interpreting it as boys' fun. He knows that Gogol is the name of a great Russian writer, but has little idea about him.

On his fourteenth birthday he receives from his father a collection of Gogol's short stories as a birthday gift. He is relieved to find little similarity between his own picture and that of the author printed on the front page of the book. For by now, he has come to hate questions pertaining to his name, hates having constantly to explain. "He hates having to tell people that it does not mean anything 'in Indian.' He hates having to wear a nametag on his sweater at Model United Nations Day at school. He even hates signing his name at the bottom of his drawings at art class. He hates that his name is both absurd and obscure, that it has nothing to do with who he is, that it is neither Indian nor American but of all things Russian." (76). He is unable to shorten his name in the way the other Indian boy in the school, Jaydeb, got people to call him Jay. For it is already short and catchy, resisting mutation. He cannot imagine any girl uttering his name under potentially romantic circumstances. It dismays him that his parents chose "the weirdest namesake." He could have lived with Leo, Anton or even Alexander, he feels. But Gogol sounds ludicrous to his ears, lacking dignity and gravity.

His intolerance with the name is severe when the teacher Mr. Lawson describes the life history of Nikolai Gogol as an introduction to his stories to be read in the class. Mr. Lawson reads out from Nikolai Gogol's biography *Divided Soul* where it is written that the writer's life, in a nutshell, was a steady decline into madness. The writer Ivan Turgenev described him as an intelligent, queer, and sickly creature. "He was reputed to be a hypochondriac and a deeply paranoid, frustrated man. He was . . . morbidly melancholic, given to fits of severe depression. He had trouble making friends. He never married, fathered no children. . . . The last years of his life were marked by physical deterioration and emotional torment . . . disillusioned and convinced of his failure as a writer, he renounced all literary activity and burned the manuscript to the second volume of *Dead Souls*. He then pronounced a death sentence on himself, and proceeded to commit slow suicide by starvation" (91). All this being too much for Gogol, he shuts his eyes and wishes he could ask Mr. Lawson to stop. He feels angry at the teacher, and also feels betrayed. The details of the author's death read out by the teacher haunt him at home and he finally decides to change his name which is a reminder of the author's suffering and his madness.

Though Gogol's American classmates in high school are dating regularly, Gogol does not date anyone and his parents do not find it strange that their son does not date. Instead they urge him to join the math team and maintain his A average. Assured by his grades and his apparent indifference to girls, his parents "did not suspect Gogol of being, in his own fumbling way, an American teenager" (93). His parents have never been on a date in their lives and they are habituated to take their behaviour as standard one, even when they are in America. They have no idea that it is absurd to think that a few months' stay in India against his will and casual observations of some Bengali rituals forced on him would develop in Gogol a sense of belonging to India.

He is rather comfortable to behave as an American and so he smokes pot and goes to spend the night at a friend's house and from there drives to a neighbouring town to see 'The Rocky Horror Picture Show.' When one Saturday he goes to a party accompanied by his friends, he meets a girl Kim and flirts with her. But he does not tell his name to Kim. He simply does not like to endure her reaction, to watch her lovely blue eyes grow wide after hearing his name. He introduces himself as Nikhil and it goes alright.

Before starting his study at Yale, he takes the trouble of riding the commuter rail into Boston, switching to the Green Line at North Station, getting out at Lechmere. He goes to the family court and on his own performs the necessary things to change his name; he decides to be known henceforward as Nikhil, the name his parents wanted to introduce in kindergarten, instead of Gogol. That night at dinner table he brings it up with his parents. He tells them that he learnt of Nikolai Gogol's lifelong suffering in the class and even accuses them of naming him after someone so strange. As he tells that he is not taken seriously because of his name, his father wants to know who does not take him seriously. Gogol knows very well that the only person who torments him, the only person "chronically aware of and afflicted by the embarrassment of his name," the only person who wishes it were otherwise, is none but he himself. Yet he lies to his father, telling him that people do not take him seriously because of his name and so the change is done.

After he is officially known as Nikhil, and becomes a student in a new place where nobody knows his earlier name, he feels that his burden that has been associated with the name Gogol is gone. He is a new person, he feels, one who is free to behave as an American boy of his age. "But now that he's Nikhil it's easier to ignore his parents, to tune out their concerns and pleas. With relief, he types his name at the tops of his freshman papers. He reads the telephone messages his suitemates leave for Nikhil on assorted scraps in their rooms. He opens up a checking account, writes his new name into course books. "Me llamo Nikhil," he says in his Spanish class. It is as Nikhil, that first semester, that he grows a goatee, starts smoking Camel Lights in parties. . . . It is as Nikhil that he takes Metro-North into Manhattan one weekend with Jonathan and gets himself a fake ID that allows him to be served liquor in New Haven bars. It is as Nikhil that he loses his virginity at a party at Ezra Stiles" (105). All these activities are gratifying: leaving the name Gogol into oblivion is suggestive of his leaving the immigrant's personality nurtured by his parents. He is now an American, living the life of an out-and-out American boy. But the outward change of life-style along with the change of his good name fails to get him metamorphosed, his mind having refused to behave as clean slate.

> There is only one complication: he doesn't feel like Nikhil. Not yet. Part of the problem is that the people who now know him as Nikhil have no idea that he used to be Gogol. They know him only in the present, not at all in the past. But after eighteen years of Gogol, two months of Nikhil feel scant, inconsequential. At times he feels as if he's cast himself in a play, acting the part of twins, indistinguishable to the naked eye yet fundamentally different. At times he still feels his old name, painfully and without warning, the way his front tooth had unbearably throbbed in recent weeks after a filling, threatening for an instant to sever from his gums when he drank coffee, or iced water, and once when he was riding in an elevator. He fears being discovered, having the whole charade somehow unravel, and in nightmares his files are exposed, his original name printed on the front page of the Yale Daily News. (105-6).

The passage quoted above clearly indicates a case of split personality. It is not that all the second-generation immigrants are supposed to develop split personality; but one like Gogol who is sensitive and introvert—for example, he is greatly moved by the names inscribed on stones in the cemetery, unlike others—cannot live in a present that has nothing to do with the past. The influence of his parents, who secretly desired their son to be an Indian at heart, cannot be wiped out from his mind in spite of his conscious efforts to be on his own. The adoption of the name Nikhil is only a gesture on his part to live only in present, but the ghost of Gogol, that is his past including the past of his parents and in some way the past of all the Indian immigrants in America, clings to him. When he signs his old name by mistake or takes time to respond when someone calls out Nikhil, he feels helpless and sometimes annoyed. He comes home during holidays obediently, but unwillingly.

Once he makes the mistake of referring to New Haven as home, much to Ashima's rage and disappointment that only three months' stay in Yale brings him to refer to New Haven as home. But to be frank with himself, he feels most comfortable in his room in Yale. He likes its oldness, its persistent grace. He likes that so many students have occupied it before him. This particular thought reveals his attempt to link him with the past of America. Consciously, he tries his best to like everything associated with the new place where he enjoys freedom. He likes the solidity of the building's plaster walls, its dark wooden floorboards, however battered and stained. "He has fallen in love with the Gothic architecture of the campus, always astonished by the physical beauty that surrounds him, that roots him to his environs in a way he had never felt growing up on Pemberton Road. For his drawing class, in which he is required to make half a dozen sketches every week, he is inspired to draw the details of buildings: flying buttresses, pointed archways filled with flowing tracery, thick rounded doorways, squat columns of pale pink stone"(108).

Gogol's desperate attempt to assert his individuality together with an adolescent's sexual urges prompted him to make a close friendship with Ruth whom he met in a crowded apartment on his way home before Thanksgiving. She tells him she was raised on a commune in Vermont, the child of hippies, educated at home until the seventh grade. Her parents are divorced now and she is going to her father who lives with her stepmother, raising llamas on a farm. Her mother, she says, is an anthropologist, doing fieldwork on midwives in Thailand. Gogol cannot imagine such a background and is thrilled at her presence. Sitting side by side they go on talking on various topics including their families. "Gogol is unaware of which state they are in, which stations they've passed. The train rumbles over a bridge; the setting sun is feverishly beautiful, casting a striking pink glow on the façades of the clapboard houses that dot the water's edge. In minutes these shades fade, replaced by the pallor that precedes dusk. When it is dark he sees that their images are reflected at an angle in the glass, hovering as if outside the train. Their throats are parched from talking and at one point he offers to go to the café car. She asks him to get her a bag of potato chips and a cup of tea with milk. He likes that she does not bother to pull the billfold out of her jeans, that she allows him to buy them for her" (111). They end up taking each other's phone number and address and meet regularly thereafter. Gogol goes to her father's farm house and enjoys the surroundings.

After almost one year, his parents know about their steady relationship, but remain indifferent without expressing any curiosity about his girlfriend. Ruth tells him she does not mind his parents' disapproval, which she finds romantic. But Gogol knows it is not right. He wishes his parents could simply accept her, as her family accepts him, without pressure of any kind. But his parents show him examples of Bengali men marrying American girls and ending in divorce. It only makes things worse when he says that marriage is the last thing on his mind. At times he hangs up on them. He pities his friends for not having experience of being young and in love. He suspects that they are secretly glad when Ruth goes away to Oxford for a semester. He is lost that spring without her. He spends all his time in the studio, especially the Friday nights and weekends he would normally have been with Ruth. It sickens him to think of the physical distance between them, to think that when he is asleep at night she is leaning over a sink somewhere, brushing her teeth and washing her face to start the next day. He longs for her as his parents have longed, all these years, for the people they love in India.[6] For the first time in his life he knows what separation means. But he does not start dating any other girl during her absence; nor does he choose a casual relationship. Instead, he waits for Ruth, thinking about her and tolerating pangs of separation. This gesture, almost an Indian one, is suggestive of the inherent Indianness in him of which his conscious mind is not aware. Unfortunately for him, his relationship with Ruth breaks down. When Ruth comes back, she praises England and other European countries so much that Gogol finds something missing. She has picked up new words and accents, typically British, and expresses her eagerness to go back to England for graduate school. Within days of being together again in New Haven, in an apartment he'd rented, they begin fighting, both admitting in the end that something is changed and that they should better keep apart. The failure of their relationship does not owe to his parents' interference, anyway. It is Gogol who fails to assess his surroundings as well as his fiancé; the idealist self that hides in his mind imagines things as perfect which are rejected by the practical outer self.

The next phase in Gogol's life starts after he has graduated from the architecture programme at Columbia and works for a firm in midtown. It's not the sort of job he'd envisioned for himself as a student. He wanted to design and renovate private residences. His advisors have told him that it is important to apprentice with big names in the beginning. And so he works with a team on designs for hotels and museums and corporate headquarters in big cities. He prefers New York, a place which his parents do not know well and which they fear.

One night he is taken to a party by one of the draftsmen at work with whom he is friendly. There he meets Maxine and very soon develops a steady relationship with her. Maxine takes him to her home and introduces Gogol to her parents, Gerald and Lydia. He observes the differences between a typical Indian immigrant's household and that of an American and prefers the latter.[7] "Quickly, simultaneously, he falls in love with Maxine, the house, and Gerald and Lydia's manner of living, for to know her and love her is to know and love all of these things. He loves the mess that surrounds Maxine, her hundreds of things always covering her floors and her bedside table, her habit when they are alone on the fifth floor, of not shutting the door when she goes to the bathroom. Her unkempt ways, a challenge to his increasingly minimalist taste, charm him. He learns to love the food she and her parents eat. . . . He learns not to put wooden spoons in the dishwasher, as he had mistakenly done one evening when he was helping to clean up" (137). This is also an idealist's approach to love, one that imagines the beloved to be perfect and is prone to disappointment at the face of any confrontation with reality. More than any thing else, Gogol appreciates the way Maxine accepts her life as it is. He is continually amazed by how much Maxine emulates her parents, how much she respects their tastes and their ways. At the dinner table she argues with them about books and paintings and people they know in common the way one might argue with a friend. There is none of the exasperation he feels with his own parents. Unlike his parents, they pressure her to do nothing, and she lives happily by their side. This aspect of American life keeps him amazed for long. So he is quietly thrilled when Maxine asks him to leave his apartment and stay in their home.

Once he starts living with Maxine and her parents in Chelsa, he is more and more aware of the differences between their way of life and that of his parents. With work as an excuse he does not go home to Massachusetts all summer. When his mother asks him to visit the following weekend, the truth seeps out of him slowly that he is going to spend a couple of weeks in New Hampshire with a girlfriend, Maxine. On the way to New Hampshire, they stop off at Pemberton Road for lunch. He knows that the sort of life which is a proud accomplishment for his own parents is of no relevance to Maxine and that she loves him in spite of it. After his short stay at home, Gogol comes to enjoy the quiet beauty of nature in New Hampshire and feels sorry for his parents who cannot relax about their physical surroundings in the way Maxine and her family do. His parents will never feel the impulse to visit a single place year after year, he knows. They have no idea of how to spend life happily, he concludes, and his entire childhood is ill spent, he feels.

Though Gogol introduces himself as an American and feels that he has no trace of Indianness in him, strangers put him in awkward position by calling him an Indian. Pamela, a neighbour of Maxine, for example, tells him in course of a conversation "you're Indian. . . . I'd think the climate wouldn't affect you, given your heritage" (157). Maxine's mother Lydia saves him this time with the explanation that he is American and he was born in America, though this information has already been given to Pamela.

Gogol spends his birthday there amidst Maxine's family; a group of guests, who has known him for only one evening, sings 'Happy Birthday.' In the midst of the laughter of these drunken persons Gogol remembers that his father left for Cleveland a week ago, that his mother is alone on Pemberton Road. He knows he should call to make sure his father has arrived safely, and to see how his mother is faring on her own. He also knows that such concerns make no sense to Maxine and her family. That night he gets out of bed as he is woken by the sound of the phone ringing and is convinced that it must be his parents' call wishing him a happy birthday. But soon he realizes that he has heard the ring in his dream. He also remembers that he has not given them the number, that he is free in this cloistered wilderness.

Gogol's relationship with Maxine is disturbed after his father's sudden death in Cleveland. The news comes to him through a phone call from Sonia when he and Maxine have returned to her parents' house at night as usual. He learns from Maxine's parents that his mother has called him twice and he feels a sting of embarrassment as he thinks that his mother being alone is habituated to call him more often. Gogol has to identify his father's dead body in a hospital in Cleveland, has to take all his belongings. He then goes to his father's apartment to vacate the rooms; he has also to call the rental office, university and many other places. Having done all this, he calls Maxine who asks him not to stay in that apartment at night. He says that he does not know anybody there and she insists on his staying in a hotel. "He is accustomed to obeying her, to taking her advice" (177). And so he dials one number for accommodation; but while he is on hold he hangs up. He does not want to go to an anonymous room. As long as he is in Cleveland, he does not want to leave his father's apartment empty. He lies on the couch in the dark, falling in and out of sleep. He thinks of his father's activities in that apartment and feels strangely vigilant, as if, "some sign of his father might manifest itself, putting a stop to the events of the day" (178).

This time a tendency to drift away from Maxine is noted in Gogol's activities and this tendency deepens day by day. A year after his father's death he feels, apart from the permanent absence of his father, "the additional absence of Maxine."

> At first she'd been patient with him, and for a while he'd allowed himself to fall back into her life, going home after work to her parents' house, to their world in which nothing has changed. Initially she had tolerated his silences at the dinner table, his indifference in bed, his need to speak to his mother and Sonia every evening, and to visit them, on weekends, without her. But she had not understood being excluded from the family's plans to travel to Calcutta that summer to see their relatives and scatter Ashoke's ashes in the Ganges. Quickly they began to argue about this, and about other things, Maxine going so far one day as to admit that she felt jealous of his mother and sister, an accusation that struck Gogol as so absurd that he had no energy to argue any more. And so, a few months after his father's death, he stepped out of Maxine's life for good" (188).

Gogol's reactions after his father's death are suggestive of the conflict between his self-cultivated American self and the latent Indian self nurtured by his parents during his boyhood.

Next time, following his mother's will, Gogol comes close to Moushumi, a daughter of Bengali immigrants, who knew him as Gogol when both of them were children. Moushumi's parents were in the friend circle of Gogol's parents, and so they had the occasion to meet, though they never became intimate that time. Moushumi, too, suffered from cross-cultural tensions, but unlike Gogol she openly protested and was without conflict in regard to her activities. She had been forbidden as a teenager to date: in her mind she would have relationships with students with whom she never spoke, with professors and TAs whom she desired silently and faithfully. But her parents and relatives had chalked out the future events of her life as per their wishes; she was always discussed by her relatives as a possible bride of some Indian groom in America and she had rebuffed the Indian men she was not interested in. She strongly protested against the system imposed on her. At first her rebellion was academic. Without telling her parents, she pursued a double major in French which was her refuge. After four years of secret study she declared that she would not be a chemist as per her parents' wish; she scraped together all the money she had and moved to Paris, with no specific plans. She began to fall effortlessly into affairs and after spending some years of free life she chose to marry an American, Graham.

When her marriage was scheduled and invitation was sent to all the relatives and friends, she came to learn that Graham only posed to be happy among her relatives in Calcutta, that he was actually irritated, and she cancelled the marriage much to the humiliation of her parents. Anyway, she marries Gogol, but the thought of changing her last name to Ganguli has never crossed her mind. Gogol does not feel jealous of her past per se, but he wonders whether he represents some sort of capitulation or defeat, for example, when he finds a tennis dress of Graham in her bag. When they go together to Paris, Moushumi is busy with her paper-reading and Gogol feels lonely. He cannot take part in the usual academic talk around the table and Moushumi's devotion to some French people, who were known to Graham, puzzles him.

One day he is hurt when Moushumi suddenly blurts out that Nikhil changed his name. "He stares at her, stunned. He has never told her not to tell anyone. He simply assumed she never would" (243). On the morning of their first anniversary it is known that she has been awarded a research fellowship to work on her dissertation in France for one year. She is happy that she is still capable of being on her own. She has genuinely liked Nikhil who obliterated her former disgrace. "And yet the familiarity that had once drawn her to him has begun to keep her at bay. Though she knows it's not his fault, she cannot help but associate him, at times, with a sense of resignation, with the very life she had resisted" (250).

Moushumi has trained herself to follow nothing but her own instincts. She is a New Woman who believes in the freedom of sex life and is not ashamed to confess it. When she starts having sex with Dimitri, Nikhil does not suspect anything in the beginning. "She wonders if she is the only woman in her family ever to have betrayed her husband, to have been unfaithful. This is what upsets her most to admit: that the affair causes her to feel strangely at peace, the complication of it calming her, structuring her day" (266). On their way to Pemberton Road, as they are going to spend the Christmas with Ashima and Sonali, Gogol learns about Moushumi's affair. As she casually refers to Dimitri, the question springs out of him if she has an affair. She tells everything and Gogol feels the anger and humiliation of having been deceived. Yet he is strangely calm. The day after Christmas she left with the excuse of a sudden interview. By the time he arrives at the apartment, all her things are gone, and she never comes back. After one year of her leaving, the shock has worn off, but a sense of failure and shame persists, deep and abiding. With an acute self-analysis, Gogol realizes that both of them have sought comfort in each other and in their shared world, perhaps for the sake of novelty, or out of the fear that that world is slowly dying. So he cannot really blame her. His time with her seems like a permanent part of him that no longer has any relevance, or currency. "As if that time were a name he'd ceased to use" (284).

During their last family gathering in the house on Pemberton Road—Ashima has decided by now to sell the house and go back to Calcutta—Gogol sits alone for sometime, thinking about the past events of their family. "In so many ways, his family's life feels like a string of accidents, unforeseen, unintended, one incident begetting another. It had started with his father's train wreck, paralyzing him at first, later inspiring him to move as far as possible, to make a new life on the other side of the world. There was the disappearance of the name Gogol's great grandmother had chosen for him, lost in the mail somewhere between

Calcutta and Cambridge. This has led, in turn, to the accident of his being named Gogol, defining and distressing him for so many years. He had tried to correct that randomness, that error. And yet it had not been possible to reinvent himself fully, to break from that mismatched name. His marriage had been something of a misstep as well. And the way his father had slipped away from them, that had been the worst accident of all, as if the preparatory work of death had been done long ago, the night he was nearly killed, and all that was left for him was one day, quietly, to go. And yet these events have formed Gogol, shaped him, determined who he is. They were things for which it was impossible to prepare but which one spent a lifetime looking back at, trying to accept, interpret, comprehend" (287). The novel ends with Gogol reading Nikolai Gogol's 'The Overcoat'—he has salvaged the collection of Gogol's stories, the book offered to him by his father as a birthday gift, by chance from the piles of books and other things to be disposed of before leaving the house for good—and this indicates a new beginning of his life.

The Namesake thus exposes the eternal quest for one's true identity in the backdrop of the cross-cultural transactions. While Ashima's portrait reveals through her experiences of long-term difficulties an anxiety to preserve an old culture in a new country, the failure of Gogol's attempt to merge into a culture reveals the possibility of a blending of two cultures through introspection and self-analysis. Gogol's interest in reading Nikolai Gogol's short stories, an interest that he develops long after he has received the book, is suggestive of his emergence from the state of self-alienation. A possible merging of two selves, namely the self of Gogol and that of Nikhil, is necessary for the process of self-analysis that Gogol undergoes to identify his real self. Ultimately, Jhumpa Lahiri highlights human conditions that transcend all borders.

Works Cited

Lahiri, Jhumpa. *The Namesake.* New Delhi: HarperCollins, 2004

NOTES

1. 'Cross-cultural Tensions: E.M. Forster and Ruth Jhabvala,' *The New Literatures in English* (New Delhi: Allied, 1985), 85-86
2. Bharati Mukherjee recognizes herself as an expatriate in Canada in *The New York Times Book Review* (1998). She says in an interview, "America, with its melting pot theory of immigration has a healthier attitude towards Indian immigrants than Canada. Although this country has its share of racial problems there are human right laws and ways to obtain legal redress in the courts," 'An Interview with Bharati Mukherjee' by Alison B. Car), *Massachusetts Review*, 29, no. 4 (1988) 652.
3. Writing as an Immigrant (New Delhi; ALR Oct-Dec. 2000),162
4. Jhumpa Lahiri in an interview, http://www.rediffmail.com/news/2000/apr/11 jhumpa.htm, p.1.
5. Lahiri points out the tensions in the life of Ashoke and Ashima and shows how they lead their children to inherit those tensions typical of the immigrants: "to a casual observer, the Gangulis, apart from the name on their mailbox, apart from the issues of *India Abroad* and *Sangbad Bichitra* that are delivered there, appear no different from their neighbours. . . . For the sake of Gogol and Sonia they celebrate, with progressively increasing fanfare, the birth of Christ, an event the children look forward to far more than the worship of Durga and Saraswati. During pujas, scheduled for convenience on two Saturdays a year, Gogol and Sonia are dragged off to a high school or a Knights of Columbus hall overtaken by Bengalis, where they are required to throw marigold petals at a cardboard effigy of a goddess and eat bland vegetarian food. It can't compare to Christmas, when they hang stockings on the fireplace mantel, and set out cookies and milk for Santa Claus, and receive heaps of presents, and stay home from school. . . . They [Ashoke and Ashima] make a point of driving into Cambridge with the children when the Apu Trilogy plays at the Orson Welles, or when there is a Kathakali dance performance or a sitar recital at Memorial Hall. When Gogol is in the third grade, they send him to Bengali language and culture lessons every other Saturday, held in the home of one of their friends"(64-65). That these attempts are unable to evoke any liking for a Bengali culture, a culture from which the children are physically and mentally separated, is not understood by the parents.

6. Gogol openly opposes the idea of feeling like an Indian immigrant. To quote from the novel, "One day he attends a panel discussion about Indian novels written in English. He feels obliged to attend; one of the presenters on the panel, Amit, is a distant cousin who lives in Bombay, whom Gogol has never met. His mother has asked him to greet Amit on her behalf. 'Technologically speaking ABCDs are unable to answer the question where are you from?' the sociologist on the panel declares. Gogol has never heard the term ABCD. He eventually gathers that it stands for 'America-born confused deshi.' In other words him. He learns that C could also stand for 'conflicted.' He knows that 'deshi,' a generic word for 'countryman,' means 'Indian,' knows that his parents and all their friends always refer to India simply as 'desh.' But Gogol never thinks of India as desh. He thinks of it as Americans do, as India." (118). That is why he could never share his parents' feelings for their relatives in India. Gogol's relationship with Ruth was the first ever serious relationship in his life and he feels the pangs of separation.
7. At dinner in Maxine's home, Gogol finds the difference between Indian culture and American culture: "Maxine lights a pair of candles. Gerald tops off the wine. Lydia serves the food on broad white plates: a thin piece of steak rolled into a bundle and tied with string, sitting in a pool of dark sauce, the green beans boiled so that they are still crisp. A bowl of small, round, roasted red potatoes is passed around, and afterward a salad. They eat appreciatively, commenting on the tenderness of the meat, the freshness of the beans. His own mother would never have served so few dishes to a guest. She would have kept her eyes trained on Maxine's plate, insisting she have seconds and then thirds. The table would have been lined with a row of serving bowls so that people could help themselves. But Lydia pays no attention to Gogol's plate. She makes no announcement indicating that there is more" (133). Gogol prefers the way Lydia manages her household.

Images of Women in *The Namesake*

TANUSHREE SINGH
RDVV, Jabalpur

Plato gives a unique definition to this world when he describes it as an image of the light of Almighty. Plato conceived a picture of a cave where a candle is burning at the centre. The light falls on one wall of the cave and then it reflects outside at the mouth of the cave. What we see in this world is not a direct impression of Almighty's light, according to Plato; it is an impression of an impression. It is twice removed from the original light. But in the end whether it is Plato's concept or the concept of *Maya* in Indian philosophy, the idea of image holds a central position in all intellectual discourse. What exactly is an image? By its very definition itself, image is not 'reality' but a reflection of the reality. Reflections can be true, they can be false. Therefore, when there is a discussion of images of people or characters in a literary work, it is essentially about the impression, the reflection and the status of a person in a social web. The image of a person is not only about how or what a person actually is; it is about the image that a person creates.

Women have always played a significant role in every society and culture, their contribution being as important as that of men. They perform several roles at different levels of their existence, in the family, home, society and nation. As fiction generally indicates the reality of everyday existence, in which women play a crucial role, the study of the images of women in fiction has become extremely important and interesting, and an indispensable part of interdisciplinary research.

With the rise of the women's movement and of feminism, many critical works have been devoted to the analysis of these images. Thus, for example, *Images of Women in Fiction*, edited by Susan Koppelman Cormillon, studies the representation of women as heroine, as the Other, and as making choices and living autonomous lives; Annis Pratt's *Archetypal Patterns in Women's Fiction* points out the archetypal images of women in western fiction; and Meena Shirwadkar in *Images of Women in Indo-Anglian Novel* traces the changes in women's images from tradition to modernity in the Indian novel in English.

It is most interesting to study the images of women in the fiction of women writers in particular, for here women represent themselves. In presenting these images women writers clearly indicate the status of women in society and their subjectivity and agency. How women see women is thus most crystalline indication of women's place in community and culture.

Jhumpa Lahiri's first and only novel *The Namesake* (2003) followed her *Interpreter of Maladies*. It too explores, like her short stories, the themes of immigrant experience, the clash of cultures and the trauma faced by the culturally displaced Indian settled in foreign countries. S. Prasannarajan in his review calls this novel "an enlarged variation of the same existential trauma of the culturally displaced that animates her debut *Interpreter of Maladies* (qtd. Ray 266).

The novel is a *Bildungsroman*, for it is primarily the story of the growing up of Gogol Ganguli, born of Bengali immigrants to the USA, who resents the way his parents cling to their 'Bengaliness' and attempts, instead to become a complete American. Gogol has been named after his father's favourite writer, Nikolai Gogol, whose famous short story "The Overcoat," he had been reading on a train journey in India. The train met with an accident and Ashoke Ganguli was saved only because the rescuers could see his book. As Gogol reaches adulthood he dislikes this pet name by which he has been known so far, and adopts his 'good name' Nikhil, much to his father's dismay. He also has American girlfriends. But when his father dies suddenly, Gogol realizes that although he is an American, he is also a Bengali. He marries an Indian American girl chosen by his mother. The marriage fails, and his mother realizes that marrying someone from the same ethnic origin does not necessarily bring about happiness.

Clearly, then, *The Namesake* also becomes the story of Gogol's mother Ashima, and the way she learns to change. Indeed, as in all Lahiri's fiction, the images of women here are central to the novel. The image of Ashima, who follows her husband to a foreign land after marriage, is that of the traditional Indian wife and mother. She suffers from the trauma of leaving behind her family and home and everything that is familiar, to accompany her husband, who is still a stranger, to a foreign land. As Smriti Singh comments:

> It is said about Indian women that they are born in an expatriate state and the movement away from home to an alien country is only an accentuation of gendered exile they have borne all along. Survival in their case is the need to survive the pain of uprooting and the 'shock of arrival.' This is followed by the struggle to surmount the obstacles and comfortably adapt to the new environment. (62)

For a large part of her life in America, Ashima feels lonely, and longs to go back to India. In the words of Indira Nityanandam, "Ashima represents the majority of women expatriates, including Indians, who are reluctant to change or to adopt the culture of the host country" (83). In doing so, she kept the faith of her grandmother alive:

> Unlike her parents, and her other relatives, her grandmother had not admonished Ashima not to eat beef or wear skirts or cut off her hair or forget her family the moment she landed in Boston. Her grandmother had not been fearful of such signs of betrayal; she was the only person to predict, rightly, that Ashima would never change. (37)

She continues to cook Indian food, wear saris, sandals from Bata and sindoor in her parting, and does not take her husband's name:

> When she calls out to Ashoke, she doesn't say his name. Ashima never thinks of her husband's name when she thinks of her husband, even though she knows perfectly well what it is. She has adopted his surname but refuses, for propriety's sake, to utter his first. It's not the type of thing Bengali wives do. Like a kiss or caress in a Hindi movie, a husband's name is something intimate and therefore unspoken, clearly patched over. (2)

She cannot understand "her children's independence, their need to keep their distance from her" (166) and feel that "she has given birth to vagabonds" (167). But Ashima also learns to change. As Uma Parameswaran comments, "Perhaps women with centuries of indoctrinations and expectations are able to adapt more quickly and to accept and love two homes without conflict or ambivalence" (qtd. Ray 7). Sonia's birth brings this about, and the land of her husband's livelihood and her children's birth becomes her home finally.

She cooks beef and American food for her children. As Gogol and Sonia leave home, Ashima even dares to live alone, when Ashoke goes to another city on work. But Ashoke dies there suddenly of a heart failure.

Ashima's initial days as a widow are lonely and sad. She has always been supported by her husband whenever she has heard a bad news of death of a loved one in India, but there is no one to support her now. Her children do give her emotional support and stand beside her, but they have their own lives to lead. After a few days they soon return to their own worlds. Ashima now feels that Ashoke's going away to Cleveland and leaving her alone was a way of "teaching me how to live alone" (183). She reaches out to non-Indian friends and her job at the library keeps her going. She no longer cooks in the old way: "She eats on the sofa, in front of the television, simple meals of buttered toast and dal, a single pot lasting her a week. . . . Sometimes she eats the way Gogol and Sonia do when they visit, standing in front of refrigerator not bothering to heat up the food in the oven or to put it on a plate" (162). Ashima is thus a survivor like Mrs. Croft of "The Third and the Final Continent" in *Interpreter of Maladies*. She decides to divide her time between America, "where her husband made his life, the country in which he died" (276) and Calcutta. Thus she will be true to her name, "True to the meaning of her name, she will be without borders, without a home of her own, a resident everywhere and nowhere" (276).

Ashima does not feel comfortable with Maxine, Gogol's girlfriend. But Maxine has a sympathetic image. She is honest and does not lie about her past relationships: "Maxine is open about her past, showing him photographs of her ex-boyfriend in the pages of a marble-papered album, speaking of those relationships without embarrassment or regret" (138). She shares a healthy relationship with her parents. They do not interfere in each other's lives. The set-up of their home is typically American. She is open-minded about other cultures. She wishes to learn about the customs and traditions of India and especially Calcutta, which is Gogol's origin. She is interested in Gogol's family and meets them with affection. Maxine's open show of affection for Gogol embarrasses Ashima and Ashoke, but this is natural to her, as is the way she addresses Gogol's parents by their names, unlike the Indian custom of addressing elders as "Uncle" or "Auntie." Ashima is stiff and uncomfortable, because of the cultural dissimilarities between them. Out of the three American girls that Gogol involves himself with, Maxine is the one who is true to him and the relationship. Gogol's identification with the American way of life and his struggle with his own identity is only reaffirmed with Maxine in his life. He realizes soon that he is more comfortable with Maxine's parents than his own. But Maxine breaks up with him as he rejects her for the sake of his family.

Ashima is interested that Gogol marries someone from his own background, and so suggests that he should meet Moushumi, whom he has known as a child. Gogol and Moushumi believe they are compatible and decide to marry. Once married however, they find that they are not matched. Moushumi is a chain smoker and Gogol soon finds himself resenting "The stale smell of it, in her hair and on her finger tips" (237). But Moushumi will not live her life according to other's expectations:

> Sometimes she would sit at a restaurant alone, at a bar, ordering sushi or a sandwich and a glass of wine, simply to remind herself that she was still capable of being on her own. This assurance is important to her; along with the Sanskrit vows she had repeated at her wedding, she'd privately vowed that she'd never grow fully dependent on her husband. (247)

She refuses to change her maiden surname and still addresses herself as Moushumi Mazoomdar. She continues being sexually promiscuous: "There were days she slept with one man after lunch, another after dinner" (215). Even though she has an understanding husband in Gogol, she soon returns to Dimitri. She is aware that what she is doing is not right: "She wonders if she is the only woman in the family ever to have betrayed her husband, to have been unfaithful" (266). Moushumi, like Rahel of *The God of Small Things*, cannot keep herself tied to a relationship; but she has a reason to cheat on Gogol; she does not love him but loves her old love Dimitri.

Sonia, Ashima's daughter is like her brother, confused between the two cultures of India and America. But as she matures and completes her studies she decides to marry Ben, her American boyfriend. She does not take very long to make up her mind to settle with Ben. Sonia's image is that of a dutiful daughter and a sister. Mira Nair's *The Namesake* has transformed Lahiri's elegant prose into celluloid. Lahiri's women in the movie are bold and independent as they are in the novel.

Some of the women of Lahiri's fiction fit into the traditional roles assigned to women. Her women do bear the burden of relationships and responsibilities to some extent, even in America, where women are supposed to be much more liberal and independent. But they do not hesitate to shed the burdens and compromise on carrying with their relationships only up to the extent of their convenience. They walk out if it does not suit them or their life style. They have the freedom of choice. Lahiri's women are survivors, because with all its faults America is known as the land of opportunity, to which the migrant goes in hope.

Works Cited

Lahiri, Jhumpa. *The Namesake*. New Delhi: Harper Collins, 2003.

Nityanandam, Indira. "Adaptation or Accommodation: Another View of the Diasporic Situation." *Jhumpa Lahiri: The Tale of the Diaspora*. New Delhi: Creative, 2005, 80-86.

Parameswaran, Uma. "Home is There Where Your Feet are and May Your Heart be There Too." *Writers of Indian Diaspora*. Ed. R.K. Dhawan. New Delhi: Prestige, 1998. 30-37.

Ray, Mohit K., Rama Kundu. *Studies in Women writers in English*. New Delhi: Atlantic, 2005.

Singh, Smriti. "Female Migrants in Divakaruni's *Arranged Marriage*." *Re-Markings,* Vol. 8, No. 1, March 2009. 61-68.

The Namesake: An Existential Novel

S.L. PAUL
Kurukshetra University, Kurukshetra

Modern literature, essentially after 1950s, is most existential. The first work of an existential text is that it underlines man's alienated self as if it were his/her inevitable condition. But it is not so, as existentialists of all hues—theistic and atheistic—- further explore, for they, beginning with Kierkegaard and Nietzsche find that man is essentially social, and indeed becomes authentic in becoming genuinely social.

Jhumpa Lahiri's *The Namesake* also tracks human inalienable urge to be part of the family and society in which one is born and has his beginning. It is in this social milieu he comes alive. However, like Ashoke and Ashima, we come to realize it only when we have deviated and departed from it, depriving us of this life-giving ambience—our social and cultural environment. The exiles actually feel it but so do those who voluntarily seek to live on a foreign strand. Alexander Pope, in one of his poems, expresses this sentiment more eloquently when he says that there cannot be a soul so dead who on coming back to one's land does not bow before it and feel once again alive.

However, as we have seen, only those know what it means to be in one's milieu who, for some reason, give up their society and choose to live among aliens, presuming that thus they make life better. Of course, they do, as do Ashoke and Ashima, in migrating to America. Ashoke had one ambition: he wanted to teach in an American university. But this ambition was of later-day origin. Initially, he was prompted by one Ghosh with whom he had a chance meeting in the train. It is what is existential in the first instance, for the central doctrine of existentialism is that 'existence precedes essence.' Ashoke's meeting with Ghosh was existential in that it was not fixed *a priori*. As Gogol later reflected, it was accidental.

In fact, human life and the working of the world—everything that happened in the novel, is contingent, happening simply by chance. In Jean Paul Sartre's terms, man is not defined by his essence—by a common quality of human nature but rather what he wills himself to be his 'thrust toward existence.' In Sartre, there is no God, a fundamental postulate of his ontology; there is no concept of man in the mind of God which constitutes man's essence. Man does not come into this world ready-made; he is simply what he makes of himself, and is never made and is always in the making.

In fact, man is his freedom; he is his choices. Of course, when he chooses for himself, he must ideally choose for others. All the same, he must bear the responsibility of his choices alone. And when Sartre says 'alone,' he means absolutely alone, for not only is there no God to share the burden, but there is no structure *a priori* for values to rest upon. Man's forlornness is his all-aloneness in which he must face the issue of his own freedom.

Lahiri's conception of human tragic-comedy is that the existential man is not only absolutely alone when it comes to choosing for himself, but he is also a creature of concerns. He is born in society and family, and he cares for it. He has no essence of his own, but gets one from his social and cultural milieu. He is simply a being there. It expresses only his existence; his essence is gained through his own efforts when he overcomes the dread of existence—his petty cares and concerns, comes to see that he is nothing—cast up between nothing and nothing, his pure being is revealed, i.e., he is ever and anon into his death.

Ashoke may not have realized these existential overtones in his life, but his life and death in America offer an abject lesson to Gogol, the namesake of Nikolai Gogol, the Russian novelist and short story writer, particularly famous for his short story 'The Overcoat.' In being named after the celebrated Russian author, Gogol, the son of Ashoke and Ashima becomes a writer himself, not that he wrote a novel but hat he becomes a chorus as it were, connecting up his parents', Sonia's and his own life in America.

Reading the flap of Gogol's book, Gogol Ganguli finds that Nikolai Gogol's chronology can be summed up briefly as follows: "Born March 20, 1809. The death of his father, 1825. Publishes his first story, 1830. Travels to Rome, 1837. Dies 1852, one month before his forty-third birthday." As we know, existentialists—Nietzsche, Heidegger and Sartre—find that death should be taken as a felicity, something to be embraced voluntarily, or preponed and even welcomed at anytime. As Heidegger says in *Being and Time*, one is always old enough to die. These existentialists think that death makes life meaningful. Most of us are inauthentic because we dread death. The existential reality of death has made man aware of his ephemeral or transitory being.

After going through the brief chronology of Nikolai Gogol, Gogol Ganguli came to reflect: "In another ten years Gogol Ganguli will be at that age [forty three]. He wonders if he will be married again one day, if he will ever have a child to name." (289) Gogol has come to know that life is ephemeral—it is there now and then lost. A month from now, he added, he would begin a new job, producing his own designs. Thus, in thinking of making a beginning, Gogol sought to take over his death by affirming himself: "There is a possibility," he thinks, "of becoming an associate, of a firm incorporating his name." And in that case, "Nikhil will live on, publicly celebrated, unlike Gogol, purposely hidden, legally diminished, now all but lost" (289-90).

Thus, Gogol decided to give up his anonymity—his name 'Gogol.' It had no legal validity. Existentialists proceed from existence, from being unknown, hidden and anonymous and wish us to become authentic—affirm ourselves with the whole of our being in every decisive moment. Gogol's father, however, returned from his being to die. He did not live in anticipation of death, as did Gogol. He said that he was born three times—as a child, in the accident and finally in America, but if you ask Gogol, his father died three times. In effect, Ashoke was afraid of death. It was his dread of his death that he named his son because he thought that it was Nikolai Gogol's book that saved him.

Ashoke also did not, at no time of his life, realize that a man's possibilities are hinted by his final end—which is always imminent. For the most part of his life, he engaged in a retreat or flight from his having to die. The train accident had shaken him. He, thereafter, lost himself in an inauthentic existence. He was so afraid that he got a security system installed at home. When Gogol brought his girl-friend Maxine and introduced her to Ashoke, the latter put up his hand as if he was about to take an oath. He did not sit down with them, but instead asked Maxine to put her car in the driveway.

Ashoke was in fact a creature of care. When Maxine said that the car was rented, he said, "It's fine where it is," but added, "but better be careful" (148). He was critical of the neighbourhood children: "They were not careful." Ashima was equally careful about things. Both of them were a worrying sort, carefully planning get-togethers; Ashima would cook everything for parties, days ahead. She would fuss about each and everything. Both of them lived an average life, acting as others—Americans or Indians—did around them. Their garage, like every other, appeared no different from their neighbours; it contained shovels, pruning shears and a sled. They purchased a barbecue for tandoori on the porch in summer. Each step, each acquisition, no matter how small, involved deliberation, consultation with Bengali friends. For the sake of Gogol and Sonia they celebrate, with progressively increasing fanfare, the birth of Christ.

Beings-in-the-world, as Heidegger would say, a world, found a home in it, and indeed displayed care of it. This is characteristic of human existence in its inauthenticity. The American world is phenomenologically revealed to them as their world, not in the sense of being the world they perceived, but as being the world they cared about, made up of things which are usable or unusable, hindrances or helps, potentially useful or potentially troublesome. Together Ashoke and Ashima never look at their world—at things—impartially—but in a certain mood—attaining themselves to it, as also at times, becoming apathetic to it, as for example, Gogol's friendship with Maxine.

But, as we have seen, acting as they do is, nonetheless, inauthentic. Except for Gogol, no one in the family is aroused out of this inauthenticity. He alone, in the end, chooses to rise out of his 'average' existence, in resolutely deciding with all his being to produce his own designs, architect as he is by training. "There is a possibility, eventually," as he contemplated, "of becoming an associate, of incorporating his name."

He resolved to leave a name behind which an average person would hardly think of. Thus, he hoped to become, a category which is in existentialism, desirable, for 'to become' entails the realization that we must die, a realization which for the novelist is of crucial importance. Gogol expressed his resolve when he was aroused out of his flat and average existence, dealing with one girl or another, for example, by his father's sudden death and the premonition of his own death. He was, as he said, already old enough to die. His namesake, the Russian writer died at the age of forty three. He would also be of the same age in a few years' time without having done anything remarkable as an authentic being. His conscience called him to do something worthy to be remembered after him. Ashima, for example, did not hear this call of conscience. She packed up and left for India.

Gogol's mind was able to hear the call of his conscience, an 'uncanny' self, as Heidegger would call it, because he, though always part of the ongoings of the world, kept himself to himself. As he thought of resolving not to live an everyday life, he knew that he would soon be distracted by his mother. Indeed, she would come upstairs where, lost in ruminations he imagined, asking him to hurry, for it was not to read a book. Gogol, had taken time off from the gathering downstairs for the last time perhaps, since his mother was leaving for India, to read Nikolai Gogol's 'The Overcoat.' And though he was not distracted by his mother, he knew that he would have to join his father's Bengali friends and families, chatter with them about his new job, clean the leftovers along with Sonia and Ben. As the hours of the evening passed, he would, he knew, grow distracted, anxious to return to his room, to be alone, to read the book he had had abandoned until then.

Traditional, Modern and Postmodern: Amalgamation in *The Namesake*

SAGAR PANDYA

Jhumpa Lahiri who is just three creations old in literary field has made her place firm by her minute eye for details and panoramic description of the characters and their background. She vividly describes each and every aspect of the story with her magic touch and that lends her creations its own colour. In spite of staying away from her native land, her novel brilliantly presents all the details that the reader wishes to find. In *The Namesake*, she presents the nice blend of traditional, modern and postmodern approach and thus succeeds in grabbing the attention of the readers.

The Namesake describes the story of an individual named Gogol who fails in accepting his odd name and tries to be detached from that ultimate reality, a fact of his life. Jhumpa Lahiri takes a complete new approach to present the identity clash of that character and manages to trap the person in his own name. Gogol realizes that his name is not Indian, where his parents belonged and nor American, where he was born. When he finds that he was named after a Russian writer Nikolai Gogol, who was an eccentric genius, deeply paranoid, frustrated man, the details of his namesake disturb him a lot and suddenly he starts hating his name more than anything else. He then realizes that Gogol was the last name of Nikolai Gogol and even he was not having the name Gogol.

The more he knows about Gogol, more he feels betrayed by his parents. The name Gogol seems funny, odd, unfit and uncharacteristic of himself. His name troubles him throughout the work and disrupts his inner being. The seemingly trivial matter causes so great a dilemma in his mind that he fails in establishing a single mature relationship with the other characters. The name 'Gogol' that he detests haunts him and spoils his sanity. He never feels like Gogol and constantly struggles to get rid of that name. For him, Gogol is a distant reality and another being. He tries to come out of the trap of that name but ends up without any success. His changing the name from Gogol Ganguli to Nikhil Ganguli too was not a relief to him. In the name Nikhil he was able to see the shadow of Nikolai and he was able to hear the echo of Nikolai in Nikhil. His search for a suitable name becomes a vital and complex thing for his personality. His parents thought that Gogol would be the pet name for their son and will be accepted was a serious mistake to which Gogol falls victim. Here they act according to Bengali tradition, in which pet name has a function to play. Jhumpa Lahiri writes, "Pet names are a persistent remnant of childhood, a reminder that life is not always so serious, so formal, so complicated. They are a reminder too, that one is not all things to all people." (26)

It indicates that an individual's identity changes from person to person and one is not the same individual to everyone. Different people perceive the personality of a character in different ways. So, in the Indian context, an individual's pet name is used by one's family members, whereas for the outside world there is the good name, a *bhalonam,* which will define an individual and provide him an identity. The awkwardness that Gogol feels with his name prevents him from taking it normally and pushes him to a point where he hates it.

Jhumpa Lahiri, especially pays more attention to the names of other characters and for what they stand for. Ashima's name means one "who is limitless, without borders" and Ashoke's name means one "who transcends grief" makes Gogol more worried for his name was a distant reality for him and also to most of the people around him, except his parents. Ashoke's naming of Gogol after a very famous writer Nikolai Gogol had some personal reasons. His attachment to this name had some deep meaning of which Gogol himself was unaware. Ashoke never realized that giving the name Gogol would create inexplicable internal conflicts in his son's life and will lead to identity crisis. Gogol fails to satisfy himself as Gogol and goes to Nikhil, a different name, to find a shelter. The sudden overnight change in his name stands in contrast with the change that his mother went through when she got married to his father and transformed herself from Ashima Bhaduri to Ashima Ganguli. She accepts that last name without any resistance and lives very comfortably. On the other hand Gogol who was named from the birth was not able to accept it. Ashima's changing of the name stands for Indian values and most of the women follow this system. The burden of having a different name carved on Gogol's life pulls him down moment-by-moment and this deterioration makes the readers also anxious. The alien-sounding name Gogol dislocates the character of Gogol and he finds no refuge anywhere. Even the name Nikhil sounded unfamiliar to him and he was not ready to be called by that name. He disturbingly asks, "Why do I have to have a new name?" (57)

There are frequent references to some Bengali cultural concepts and landmarks of Kolkata that provide it an Indian touch. Throughout the novel, Jhumpa Lahiri keeps bringing the native connection alive. She writes about College Street from which Ashoke used to buy the books and hints about an actress Madhabi Mukherjee. The life style that an American lady Mrs. Jones enjoys stands in contrast with the life that Ashoke's mother enjoys in India. This is described as a life of humiliation. Jhumpa Lahiri writes, "Mrs. Jones leads a life that Ashoke's mother would consider humiliating: eating alone, driving herself to work in snow and sleet, seeing her children and grandchildren, at most, three or four times a year." (48)

When Ashima and Ashoke were abroad they maintained their Indian connection intact. The couple was able to remain rooted in spite of all American surroundings. Their 'Bong Connection' never loosens even when the conditions were difficult. She never spoke the name of her husband and behaves like a faithful wife. Jhumpa Lahiri writes, "Like a kiss or caress in Hindi movie, a husband's name is something intimate and therefore unspoken, cleverly patched over." (2)

Ashima, in spite of being a traditional wife, knows how American people used to live and according to that she also manages to live. She adjusts herself in an alien country and tries to live happily. She feels that "Americans, in spite of their public declarations of affection, in spite of their miniskirts and bikinis, in spite of their hand-holding on the street and lying on top of each other on the Cambridge Common, prefer their privacy" (3).

The Namesake is a story of Ashoke, Ashima and Gogol's life told in a very simple manner presenting a conflict that seems very mild on surface but had the capability to disturb an individual. Gogol's search for identity ultimately ends with some sort of satisfaction to him and relieves him. *The Namesake* comes across as a nice blend of traditional, modern and post modern approach that the writer takes up and successfully sums up.

Work Cited

Lahiri, Jhumpa. *The Namesake*. India: HarperCollins, 2003.

Bibliography

Apte, Sudhir. "*The Namesake*." 7.Sept., 2003. MostlyFictionBookReviews. Ed. Judy Clark. Web. 24 Nov., 2009. <http://www. mostlyfictioncom/world/lahiri.htm>

Ashcroft, Bill, Gareth Griffiths and Helen Tiffin. *Key Concepts in Postcolonial Studies*. London: Routledge, 2004.

Bhattacharya, Atanu. "Relocating the Diasporic Space," *Interpreting Indian Diasporic Experience*. Ed. Adesh Pal. New Delhi: Creative, 2004.

Caldwell, Gail. *Globe.com*. n.d. Web. 12 Sept. 2009.

Das, Subhamoy. "Jhumpa Lahiri on her Debut Novel: An Interview with the Author." *Hinduism Today*. Mifflin Houghton Books. N.d. Web. 5 Oct. 2009.

Desai, R.W. "Catering to the West through Stereotypes: Some Relections on Bharati Mukherjee and Jhumpa Lahiri." *New Concerns: Voices in Indian Writing*. Delhi: Macmillan India, 2006. 73-84.

Forster, E.M. *Aspects of the Novel*. Harmondsworth, U.K.: Penguin, 1927, Reprint 1968.

Hartley, John. *Key Concepts in Communication, Cultural and Media Studies*. London: Routledge, 2004.

Hallgren, Sherri. "The Namesake." Post-gazette.com. Web. 5 Oct. 2003. Web. 23 Sept. 2009. <post-gazettel.com/books/reviews/ 20031005 lahiri 1005fnp 6.asp>

Hore, Rachel. "Jhumpa Lahiri: Writer in search of roots." *Sunday Tribune*. Chandigarh (By arrangement with the *Independent*). June 29, 2008.

Kakutani, Michiko. Kirkus Reviews. "Jhumpa Lahiri." 1 Feb. 2008. Web. 15 Sept. 2009 <randomhouse.com/kvpa/jhumpalahiri/review s.php>

Lahiri, Jhumpa. *The Namesake*. New Delhi: Harper Collins, 2003.

Leech, Geoffrey N. & Michael H. Short. *Style in Fiction*. London: Longman, 1981.

Misra, Lalji & Richa Misra. "Bharati Mukherjee: A Diaspora Novelist." *The Indian Journal of English Studies* (2005-06). 147-58.

Mukherjee, Bharati. An Interview by Alison, B. Car. *Massachusetts Review*, 29, no. 4 (1988) 652.

Nahal, Chaman. "Cross-cultural Tensions: E.M. Forster and Ruth Jhabvala." *The New Literatures in English.* New Delhi: Allied, 1985, 85-86.

Nandan, Satendra, "Diasporic Consciousness." *Interrogating Postcolonial Theory, Text and Context.* Ed. Harish Trivedi & Meenakshi Mukherjee. Shimla: Indian Institute of Advanced Studies, 1996.

Nityanandam, Indira. "Adaptation or Accommodation: Another View of the Diasporic Situation." *Jhumpa Lahiri: The Tale of the Diaspora.* New Delhi: Creative, 2005, 80-86.

Owens, Jill. "Telephonic Interview with Jhumpa Lahiri." *Powell's.com.* April 4, 2008. Web. 20 Sept. 2009.

Pal, Adesh, ed. *Theorizing and Critiquing Indian Diaspora.* New Delhi: Creative, 2004.

—. *Interpreting Indian Diasporic Experience.* New Delhi: Creative, 2004.

Parameswaran, Uma. "Home is There Where Your Feet are and May Your Heart be There Too." *Writers of Indian Diaspora.* Ed. R.K. Dhawan. New Delhi: Prestige, 1998. 30-37.

Ray, Mohit K., Rama Kundu. *Studies in Women writers in English.* New Delhi: Atlantic, 2005.

Rushdie, Salman. *Imaginary Homelands.* London: Granta Books, 1992.

Shanghvi, Siddharth Dhanvant. "The Betrayal Artist." New Delhi: *Sunday Times of India,* April 20, 2008.

Sharma, J.C. Inaugural Address. "Indian diaspora: Responsibilities and Relationships, Strengths, Weaknesses and Contribution." *Theorizing and Critiquing Indian Diaspora.* Ed. Adesh Pal.

Sherif, Chouhette. "Book Review: *The Namesake.*" 3 March, 2007. Web. 18 Oct. 2009. <http://www.Istbookreview.com/2007/03/nameake_by_jhumpa_lahiri.html>

Shrivastava, Prem. "Literature Still Matters! *The Namesake*: Woman Reads Woman." *Contemporary Fiction: An Anthology of Female Writers.* Ed. Vandana Pathak et al. New Delhi: Sarup & Sons, 2008. 28-47.

Sidhwa, Bapsi. "Writing as an Immigrant." New Delhi: ALR Oct-Dec. 2000,162.

Singh, Smriti. "Female Migrants in Divakaruni's *Arranged Marriage.*" *Re-Markings,* Vol. 8, No. 1, March 2009. 61-68.

Teresa, Wiltz. "The Writer who began with a hyphen: Jhumpa Lahiri between two cultures." Bookrags.com. 10 Aug. 2003. Web. 8 Nov. 2009.